CARTHA – *On The Form of Form* was developed for the 2016 Lisbon Architecture Triennale as an Associated Project. Issues I, II and II of the cycle were presented in Lisbon in two exhibitions held at Mãe d'Água das Amoreiras during October and December 2016 as part of the official program of the Triennial.

The origin of this book dates back to the autumn of 2016, when the Lisbon Architecture Triennale was held under the motto of *The Form of Form.* This tautological expression derived from what Diogo Seixas Lopes (1972–2016) and I thought would be the most crucial question to discuss at a time when Europe was struggling with all manner of political and cultural dilemmas. Under the continuing financial constraints of our era, architecture seemed to be gradually transforming into a mere technical service for embellishing the physical results of economic policies. At the same time, architectural critics and institutions were becoming entangled in radical arguments that were difficult to combine with our day-to-day practice. How can we ensure that architecture is recognized as a cultural practice? How can we ensure that architecture is considered to be a type of knowledge that will continue to be deployed amidst all of the world's contradictions? This was the task we proposed under the scope of the Triennale program, knowing that the challenge went way beyond architecture; the difficulty lies in being able to restore a general recognition of culture as one of the main social forces.

The Form of Form was an obvious title for architects who see the world through built forms. It was far removed from formalism, as each form embodies all of its own underlying material and social complexities; it was as if form, over and above its reality, served as a pretext for discussing what we do as architects, for questioning how we deal with all the social, economic, legal, technical and ethical challenges we face as individuals. This hypothesis underlay the development of a program that included a number of exhibitions intended to generate a dialogue. The dialogue was designed to take place in Lisbon – in a place where a major urban transformation was just starting, and at a time when a severe economic and social crisis seemed to have been overcome – but our aim was to involve fellow architects from all over the world, taking advantage of the city and its citizens as a resourceful milieu and, in return, providing them with as many ideas and discussions as we could bring from abroad. It was in this context that a group of young architects took part in the programme, inviting us to join in the debate with a plethora of arguments, doubts, possibilities, expectations and dreams.

CARTHA made an exciting contribution to *The Form of Form* program. By examining many of the questions arising on its margins, CARTHA expanded the content presented at the main exhibitions and satellite programmes, bringing forth new ideas and hypotheses and opening up dialogues with themes and contents that we had been neglecting. Its experience with an open network of engaged contributors guaranteed the inclusion of a wide range of emerging voices and arguments, but not without also generating a number of occasional but fruitful controversies. Overwhelmed by the demands of the main programme, we could not have been more grateful to CARTHA, which brought added interest and liveliness to our architectural discussions in Lisbon.

When these sometimes heated discussions are transposed to books, they seem to lose some of their passion in favor of greater order and reason. This loss, or this gain, sheds different lights on its various contents. The reflections of the still water on the limestone, the memory of Lisbon's reservoir of plain architecture, are no longer there. Instead, it becomes possible to grasp each idea more clearly, viewing it in line with new discussions and arguments and discarding previous hypotheses. Another function of the book is simply to serve as a memory: operating in parallel to the main program, most of the contents that CARTHA brought to *The Form of Form* were ephemeral, so that the book reproduces the memory of what was discussed and redistributes it for our consideration over the long term. It can therefore be read in the company of *The Form of Form's* other publications, reflecting the various positions that were adopted in another time and place. But the book form, which requires a precise protocol and a strict editorial discipline, also serves to underline what was our main expectation when we initiated *The Form of Form* programme. Architecture is a form of culture, a kind of knowledge that has to be performed. Architecture is activated through construction, but requires great intellectual commitment in order to retain its cultural potential. With all of its multiple positions, this book performs architecture.

> André Tavares, Co-Chief Curator of the 2016 Lisbon Architecture Triennale
> with Diogo Seixas Lopes

Architecture is the image of a society turned into geometry, into an inhabitable form.
It turns the idea into form and the form into a dwelling.
Octavio Paz

In 2016, CARTHA was selected as an Associated Project of the Lisbon Triennale of Architecture, and adopted the topic of the triennale, *The Form of Form,* as its theme for the 2016 yearly editorial cycle.

Addressing *The Form of Form* worked as a counterpart to the first cycle, On Relations in Architecture, approaching architecture not through the intangible network of relations that enables it to exist, but rather through the set of concepts and ideas that dictate what form is and how we understand it in its different scales, scenarios and contexts.

CARTHA – On *The Form of Form* was composed of three issues. The first was headed by guest editor Bureau A and the second was guest edited by Victoria Easton, Matilde

Cassani and Noura Al Sayeh. Their participation in this cycle allowed CARTHA to widen its scope on the topic by adopting the take of the guest editors on the cycle's theme, and to enrich the set of confluent editorial intentions within the whole cycle. The third issue was edited solely by CARTHA's editorial board.

All issues share the use of a historical reference model to conceptually and formally frame their content and structure. The works *How to Work Better* by Fischli and Weiss, *The Architecture of the City* by Aldo Rossi, and *Roma Interrotta,* conceived by Piero Sartogo, served as a basis for each of the three issues, respectively. Revisiting these pivotal works provided valuable tools in the cycle's journey through form.

How to Learn Better, edited in collaboration with Bureau A, inaugurated the cycle by questioning the learning methods around architectural production and the conceptualization of form. Through a series of posters, a wide spectrum of different personalities ranging from architects, to artists, writers, photographers and graphic designers, contributed with their unique visions on learning, producing in nine contributions a variety of divergent positions on the pedagogy of architecture. By having almost half of the contributions produced by non-architects, a window into several different experiences and contexts opened up, expanding through a process of coding and decoding the questions around architecture pedagogy as genesis of form. With these nine posters, CARTHA and Bureau A pose a simple question: How to learn better?

Shifting from the discussion of the pedagogical origins of architectural form, the second issue focused on the form of the city through a palimpsest of Aldo Rossi's *The Architecture of the City.* The proposal by guest editors Victoria Easton, Matilde Cassani and Noura Al

Sayeh, was framed as a necessary exercise in a moment where drastic changes in the way we read and form the city make it necessary to question the current state of architecture, paralleling Rossi's questioning of the Modernist doctrine in 1966. This palimpsest proved that the ideas embodied through Rossi's original 33 chapters are as valid and lucid as they were 50 years ago. Their flexibility and, at times, ambiguity provided a fertile soil for reflections that not only seem pertinent but also urgently necessitated by the contemporary city. Reflecting on form through the revisiting of Rossi's oeuvre enriches our cycle on *The Form of Form,* suggesting another way in which form and architecture relate, while pointing to the final issue of the cycle.

Concluding the cycle, reflections on the form of cities intertwine in *Lisboa Paralela.* The issue consists of two complementary sets of contributions: one based on Piero

Sartogo's *Roma Interrotta,* where instead of Rome, Lisbon served as a base for a selected group of international architects to design and re-interpret a stripe of the current city. Based on *parallel realities,* without social, political or natural restraints of any kind, the results show the unimpeded character of these architects and force us to look at Lisbon through their eyes, speculating on the present and perceiving it with renewed attention.

In addition, a series of contributions resulting from an open call for papers, takes us into similar journeys, expanding the reach of the issue beyond Lisbon's borders.

Alongside the online issue, the cycle contemplated the exhibition *CARTHA – On The Form of Form,* featured at the Mãe d'Água das Amoreiras as part of the official program of the 2016 Lisbon Architecture Trienniale. The exhibition contained three issues of the cycle : *How to Learn Better, Architecture of the City. A Palimpsest* and *Lisboa Paralela* were exhibited.

With three issues that vary significantly in format, the cycle presents a set of suggestions on how to approach form from different perspectives and with dissimilar goals. It raises questions and allows the inference of answers, but it contains no certainties. It remains open and ripe with possibilities for further interpretation while containing a clear message regarding its relevance to the contemporary moment.

CARTHA Editorial Board

13 How to L

earn Better

Editorial
Bureau A

HOW TO LEARN BETTER is an issue on architectural education and learning. Inspired very intimately by the writings of Richard Sennet *The Craftsman* and *Together,* this number of the CARTHA series explores how an architect is or can be educated and what are the milestones of the architect's learning progression. What are the skills he or she must develop, and how can these skills be useful – or not – in a professional world?

Education is probably the most influential moment in an architect's career, when the beginning of a creative identity emerges and starts pointing out particular interests and fields of exploration that will constitute later, in a professional journey, the specificity of every practice. We thus believe that this moment, those years of learning, are of incredible importance, where the amount of cultural discovery is balanced by the formation and definition of specific personalities. Despite the fact that the process of learning clearly does not end with the end of studies, the first impulse is launched during those university years and will drive the continuous learning process.

The other aspect of education that seems quite intriguing is the variety of educational typologies that have prevailed for the past 100 years or so, from Beaux-Arts-oriented schools to what Beatriz Colomina has named *Radical Pedagogies* (implemented by schools such as Black Mountain College in the 1930s). It is very curious to admit that the education imparted by all of these very different institutions provides more or less the same professional title. We are thus forced to admit that architecture can hardly be considered an homogeneous discipline. Or shall we draw the conclusion that the definition of the skills that an architect must have is so vague that it can be achieved through a wide diversity of educational paths?

Yet, the education of an architect calls for tools, and these tools make him or her skilled. Drawing, writing, model-making, photography and filming are indispensable tools that the architect will use throughout his professional life to accomplish his projects, to materialize his or her ideas.

Richard Sennett's writings have focused on craft and making. His trilogy *Homo Faber* (from which the two first volumes have been written) deals with the relation of man to things. How can mankind relate to a physical world of made things and what are the tools and skills needed to materialize this relationship? The philosophical background of this question is not negligible: can we even think or name one thing without having experienced it physically? Can the idea of an object appear before its physical existence?

In the second volume of his trilogy, *Together,* the sociologist develops the notion of collaboration as opposed to solidarity, where a bottom-up human activity achieves highly efficient and qualitative levels of production.

The relation to THE FORM OF FORM – this year's theme for the Lisbon Triennale of Architecture – is thus a logical consequence of this same thinking. How can we talk about FORM without discussing the form of WHAT? And how can WHAT be defined without a physical reference? And then, this is where the physical reference is rooted, in the CONTEXT that produces it, that allows its emergence. And finally, WHO makes, within this context, the WHAT that addresses a FORM? We strongly believe that forms cannot be discussed outside this complex system and that form does not exist as an object, even as a conceptual one. Within the context of the Triennale, the question would then be: from what moment of the learning journey of an architect can form be discussed?

When does this question becomes important, if it does?

HOW TO LEARN BETTER wants to address these issues through a pictorial approach. The words and sentences are painted, made out of collage of from a graphic design approach, like definite slogans that address the issue of learning architecture. This pictorial approach presents the learning process in its relationship to methodology. The written/painted words or sentences are a condensed broth of an educational theory.

22 Embrace Fiction
233 Luis Úrculo

24 Notes on Conceptual Learning in Architecture
228 Andrea Alberto Dutto
233 Carolin Stapenhorst

26 Untitled
227 Amateur Cities

28 Critique of the Jouissance Reason
230 Tristan Lavoyer
Dimitri de Preux (Translation)

30 Education
227 Titi Balali
230 Manuel Krebs
233 Shirana Shahbazi

32 Untitled
Farquet Architectes:
228 Grégoire Farquet
229 Eric Leo Gösswald
229 Anna Katharina Hüveler

34 Excercices de style
226 Åbäke

36 Untitled
229 Sam Jacob

38 TOGETHER : The Rituals, Pleasures and Politics of Cooperation
228 ALICE: Dieter Dietz

22 Embrace Fiction

233 Luis Úrculo

EMBRACE FICTION

Notes on Conceptual Learning in Architecture

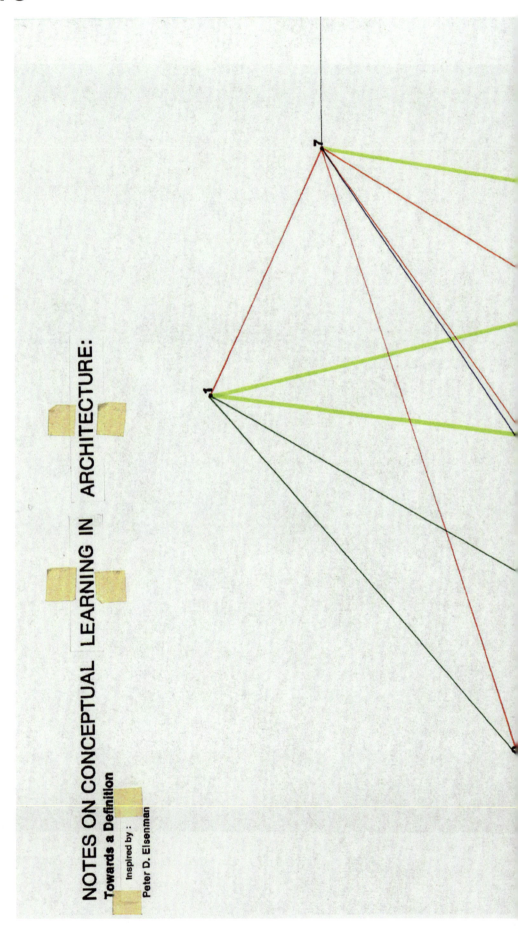

NOTES ON CONCEPTUAL LEARNING IN ARCHITECTURE:
Towards a Definition

Inspired by:
Peter D. Eisenman

Andrea Alberto Dutto
Carolin Stapenhorst

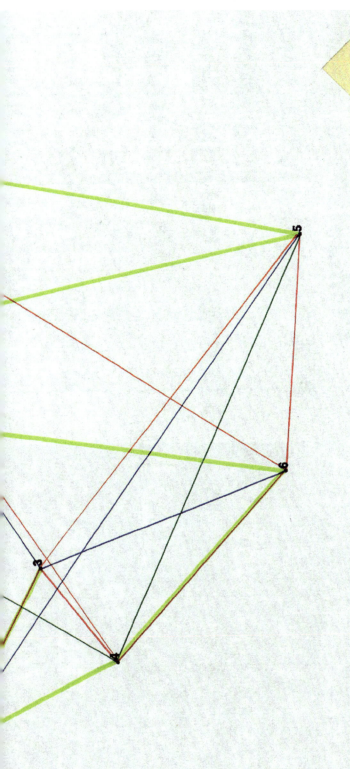

1. "Bring the intelligent points of a scheme immediately before the eyes [...]." Cfr. Le Corbusier, *The heart of the city: towards the humanisation of urban life* ed. by J. Tyrwhitt, J. L. Sert, E. N. Rogers, Humphries, London, 1952.

2. "When one is face to face with an actual problem, the mass of material is very complicated. One has to put this in order, and therefore one proceeds to construct a mental architecture amid the chaos." Cfr.Le Corbusier, "Use of the Grid as a "thinking tool"", ed. by [...], Le Corbusier, *The heart of the city: towards the humanisation of urban life* ed. by J. Tyrwhitt, J. L. Sert, E. N. Rogers, Humphries, London, 1952.

3. "Your silent problem lie displayed immediately before your eyes, and their environment is spread out before you ." Cfr. Le Corbusier, *The heart of the city: towards the humanisation of urban life* ed. by J. Tyrwhitt, J. L. Sert, E. N. Rogers, Humphries, London, 1952.

4. "A program is always based on a multiplicity of references and from this point of view it is the real premise to the multiplicity and complexity of the architectural figure." Cfr. Motta G., Pizzigoni A., *L'orologio di Vitruvio. Introduzione a uno studio della macchina di progetto*, Edizioni Unicopli, Milano, 1998.

5. "[...] which is providing us with these protective rules - resemblance, contiguity, causality - which enable us to put some order into ideas." Cfr. Deleuze G., Guattari F., "Conclusion: From Chaos to the Brain", *What is Philosophy?*, Verso, London/New York, 1994.

6. "Irrational thoughts should be followed absolutely and logically." Cfr. Lewitt S., "Sentences on Conceptual Art" in *0 to 9*, New York, 1969.

7. "If the artist wishes to explore his idea thoroughly, then arbitrary or chance decisions would be kept to a minimum, while caprice, taste and others whimsies would be eliminated from the making of the art." Cfr. Lewitt S., "Paragraphs in Conceptual Art" in *Artforum*, New York, June 1967.

Untitled

OPINION MATTERS
DON'T CREATE USELESS TASKS FOR OTHERS
ARCHITECTURE IS NOT NEUTRAL. OBJECTS HAVE POLITICS
DON'T TALK ABOUT YOUR WORK DESCRIPTIVELY
A MODEL IS NOT A BUILDING
PUT STUFF ON PAPER
TEST AND MAKE THINGS.
YOUR IDEAS MAY AFFECT PEOPLE'S LIVES (FOR BETTER OR WORSE)
COLLABORATE
DON'T OVERANALYZE IT. THE POINT IS TO CHANGE THE WORLD, NOT TO EXPLAIN YOUR IDEAS

Amateur Cities

MAKER

master

In love there are
no professionals.
Ask stupid questions.
Read newspaper
sections you don't
find interesting.
Make time for
other things.
Appreciate small
achievements.

THINKER

amateur

Respect your
teachers
Learn from
the past
Listen to yourself,
Spend time alone
Good intentions
are not enough.
Developing skills
takes time & patience

Critique of the Jouissance Reason

Alice is tired, she has cuckolded her husband and she's afraid. Her forest epic which happened during her childhood has plunged her into an ubiquity. She tells herself that it's easy to omit her act by way of her daydreams that take her to the very unavowed place of her madness — to sleep once again with the logician, she loves him so much — and to spend her time performing a daily blah-blah between expression and repression. Her husband, elegant but dumb, Ulysses that is, doesn't know how to arouse her/his imagination. Besides, he stands in another epoch, between the sidewalk of Mexico City and Kafka's character K. Yet, every now and then, taken by a surge of lucidity given his young age, he repeats his own proper noun to himself. Alice walks around, her tra-

Knowledge, if it exists, finds its meaning within organisms in trance, away from the snubs of cynicism. Knowledge sharpens us for the appetite of indefinite spaces. These spaces are neither against us, nor against myself, nor beyond these two instances, but are a materialist idealism. Yes, put another way, when I speak with Alice she always lets me look on and in the cave and tells me about her findings. Ulysses lets himself go towards the passerby, the one who is looking down on him and for whom he dedicates his finger, palm, arm and body. However, you could blame me for it, Alice and Ulysses, even though you know them and explore them, are the fruits of one imagination and one reality. This is certainly not the case, Alice and Ulysses are at times myself and the

I should explain the function of the parable, to ensure a clear understanding about what is reductive and moralizing about the metaphor when it brings two objects to a single dialectical entity in order to systemize them. Alice and Ulysses are in a clash against the rational beasts, these things as they are called, which in their proselytizing surges fabricate metaphors in order to associate the technical elements (their bodies) to an effectivity of meaning (their concrete form). They're certainly dissidents, where their existence flaps through explications by which things force themselves to bring them back.

The daily blah-blah, ultimately, turns out to be Perec's *Things*, *Les Choses* in French, this moment when the

Beautiful existence, beautiful ruse, Alice and Ulysses, you who aimed at foiling reality, you are the poor children of these conquerors. These rational beasts have transformed you into the disabled of judgement and have finally caught you between the lethargic cosmos and the unconscious frenzy, in their unbounded speculation. Our two characters have understood that meaning isn't actually concrete, but that it's a sort of post-cultural fertilizer circulating between and within the legislating organs. But what's fun is to be outside inside the system which bounds you to the thing and which really wants to make us come, at least in the common bowl. We can, if we want, reinvent our life excessively, modify the organ which brought into being the bosom of your sexualiza-

Tristan Lavoyer
Dimitri de Preux (Translation)

CRITIQUE OF THE JOUISSANCE REASON

where one can observe how planes take off at different paces above the garden's tree. The problem of Ulysses ; one has to pierce the ceiling, he tells himself.

- AAAh Alice, says Ulysses.
- UUUh Ulysses, says Alice.

justify. Well actually, Alice and Ulysses are precisely the moment when the justification transforms itself into an action estranged from a will to be. Vague and free comets above our sound and laden skies and earths.

The lyrical musing these people are capable of is the moment when the ultra-conscience about a system has been achieved, but, paradoxically, the abolition of which is made impossible.

which produce, from time to time, restlessness. Many skillful means have enabled Ulysses and Alice to get rid of the thing. Love, sex and boredom, and most of all, to build of a dense dump, that is to say, to plunge into the very object of the thing's incapacity. Otherwise, I take hold of the thing and of my body's phenomenology, and wham, here I am, the professional who masters this process which makes the object blossom, very often, a big Bertha, in other words, a cop and a banger.

Yet, it's only organization which is of interest for the two lovers, a kidney, a liver, a heart, and other limbs that mate, separate, and offset the loss of energy to this fascist-like and systematic reality that isn't concrete. That's the metaphor of an existence turned on itself, of what Marx gently termed alienation and for which the only solution Ulysses and Alice found is the undeniable dereliction devoid of content and form, anti-discourse.

nicality of the word converges with the language of Homer. Despite this diminish view, Ulysses and Alice are exceptional people, of short stature, lilliputians who move laboriously and appreciate the roadside built by the giants. They aren't married, they haven't any children, they don't know who they are, they deny the reality principle. They don't know about microwaves, they never heard about custard pies, they aren't familiar with Antiquity, and more generally, they ignore history, they ignore death, etc.

30 Education

SMALL EDUCATION B1 — *SOCIAL SKILLS*

SEVEN SHORT LESSONS ON HOW TO EXPRESS YOURSELF ADEQUATELY IN CONVERSATION

REMEMBER THAT NOWADAYS, EVERY CONVERSATION IS A JOB INTERVIEW.

↑

1. REMEMBER CLARITY.
   ALWAYS SPEAK SLOWLY AND CLEARLY. PRETEND YOU'RE TALKING TO AN ARTIST.
2. REMEMBER TO MAKE TRANSITIONS.

- (227) Titi Balali
- (230) Manuel Krebs
- (233) Shirana Shahbazi

3. REMEMBER THE HUMOR.
HUMOR BEGINS WITH THE CHOICE OF WORDS. KNOW WHICH WORDS ARE FUNNY AND WHICH WORDS ARE NOT. ALKA SELTZER IS FUNNY. YOU SAY 'ALKA SELTZER' YOU GET A LAUGH. WORDS WITH 'K' IN THEM ARE FUNNY. CASEY STENGEL, THAT'S A FUNNY NAME. ROBERT TAYLOR IS NOT FUNNY. CUPCAKE IS FUNNY. TOMATO IS NOT FUNNY. COOKIE IS FUNNY. CUCUMBER IS FUNNY. CAR KEYS. CLEVELAND. IPSO FACTO. CRITIC/CURATOR. POSTCOLONIAL. POSTCOLONIAL IS FUNNY. MARYLAND IS NOT FUNNY. THEN THERE'S CHICKEN. CHICKEN IS FUNNY. PICKLE IS FUNNY. INTERDISCIPLINARITY IS NOT FUNNY. SOMEONE ACTUALLY RESEARCHED WHY THE 'K' SOUND IS FUNNY: IT HAS SOMETHING TO DO WITH THE SOUNDS WE ASSOCIATED WITH COMFORT AS BABIES. LIKE COOTCHIE-COO. CUDDLE. COZY. ETC. BUT THE CHOICE OF WORDS ASIDE. HUMOR HINGES ON THE PUNCHLINE. THE PUNCH-LINE GETS ITS NAME FROM THE DELIVERY TECHNIQUE. YOU MUST PUNCH THE LINE OUT A LITTLE HARDER AND WITH A SLIGHTLY DIFFERENT VOICE THAN THE REST OF THE JOKE. SAY IT LOUDER AND MORE CLEARLY THAN YOU SAID THE SETUP LINES. JUST BEFORE THE PUNCHLINE YOU SHOULD PAUSE SLIGHTLY TO EMPHASIZE AND DRAW SPECIAL ATTENTION TO THE LINE. ALSO, DELIVER THE LINE TO ONE PERSON AND ONE PERSON ONLY. THE PERSON TO WHOM YOU DELIVER THE PUNCHLINE IS NOT RANDOMLY CHOSEN. I DELIVER PUNCH LINES TO A PERSON I KNOW IS GOING TO LAUGH. HOW DO I KNOW? I PAY ATTENTION. THAT'S HOW I KNOW.

4. REMEMBER THE GESTURES.
THE LARGER THE GROUP, THE LARGER AND SLOWER THE GESTURES. IF YOU HAVE A SMALL GROUP, USE SMALLER GESTURES. GENERALLY, LET YOUR WORDS TRIGGER YOUR ACTIONS. IF YOU ARE COUNTING, HOLD OUT YOUR FINGERS. IF YOU SAY NO, SHAKE YOUR HEAD NO. HOLD YOUR HANDS OPEN AND WIDE APART TO SHOW SINCERITY AND HONESTY. HOLD YOUR HANDS BEHIND YOUR BACK WHEN ASKED A QUESTION (BUT DON'T OVERDO IT). ALSO AVOID EXCESSIVE HANDS IN POCKETS, CLENCHED FISTS, POINTING, HANDS ON HIPS, AND THE INFAMOUS FIG LEAF POSITION WHERE YOUR HANDS ARE CROSSED IN FRONT OF YOUR GROIN.

5. REMEMBER THE COMPETITION.
DO NOT HESITATE TO BLOW OUT OTHER PEOPLE'S CANDLES TO MAKE YOURS SHINE BRIGHTER. IF YOU DO IT WELL, NO ONE WILL NOTICE.

6. REMEMBER HOW TO CLOSE A CONVERSATION.
IF THE SUBJECT IS APPROPRIATE, HUMOROUS CLOSINGS ARE PREFERABLE FOR SEVERAL REASONS. IF YOU LEAVE THEM LAUGHING, AN EXTREMELY POSITIVE IMPRESSION ABOUT YOU WILL REMAIN. THE SAME SHIFT IN TECHNIQUE CAN BE VERY EFFECTIVE IN ENDING A MOSTLY HUMOROUS ENGAGEMENT. HAVE THEM LAUGHING ALL ALONG WHILE YOU MAKE YOUR POINTS. THEN FINISH SERIOUSLY. THIS CONTRAST WILL CREATE A GREAT IMPACT. IT WILL CONVEY THE FACT THAT YOU BELIEVE IN A LIGHTHEARTED APPROACH TO THE SUBJECT, BUT THE RESULTS ARE VERY SERIOUS TO YOU.

7. REMEMBER TO REVISE.
MAKE A TRANSCRIPT OF YOUR CONVERSATIONS, WHICH YOU CAN RECORD WITH A STANDARD DIGITAL VOICE RECORDER. HOW DID YOU FARE? DID YOU SEEM DULL, INSECURE, OR SELF-INDULGENT? HERE'S AN EXERCISE: CIRCLE EVERY 'I' AND EVERY 'YOU' THAT YOU HAVE UTTERED. WHAT'S THE RATIO? IF IT'S NOT THREE TO ONE IN FAVOR OF 'YOU', REWRITE YOUR CONVERSATION.

32 Untitled

Farquet Architectes:
- 228 Grégoire Farquet
- 229 Eric Leo Gösswald
- 229 Anna Katharina Hüveler

34 Excercices de style

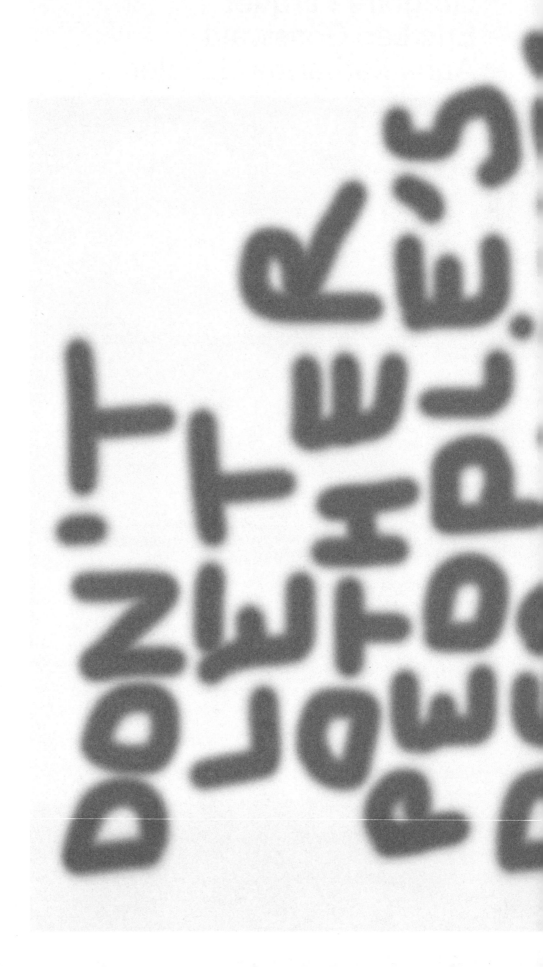

Åbäke

Untitled

Sam Jacob

38 TOGETHER : The Rituals, Pleasures and Politics of Cooperation

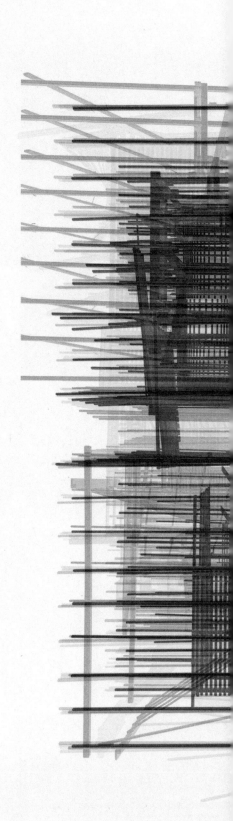

HOUSE I

ALICE: Dieter Dietz

41 Ⓘ Ⓘ Ⓘ
Architectur
City. A Palin

(IV) The Rise of the Palimpsest

- (43) Editorial
- (228) Victoria Easton
- (227) Matilde Cassani
- (226) Noura Al Sayeh

Tout est forme, et la vie même est une forme.
Honoré de Balzac

While teaching a child how to put little wooden volumes into correspondent holes, one could consider form as an absolute given. However, the tautological title *Form of Form* suggests intrinsic transformability and hints at a construct in constant change, which we will here interpret as the city. Smart, participative, green, segregating, gentrifying, polluting, museified, ideal: the city orchestrates our daily life. The city, this inexplicable phenomenon, best incarnates moldable form, or simply is form.

Enough has been written about the urban phenomenon, and our ambition here does not lie in a one-of-a-kind reassessment of this topic. On the contrary, we consider one book to be one of the best commentaries on the city, its actors and its realm. Roughly 50 years ago, Aldo Rossi wrote his seminal text *The Architecture of the City* and suggested in the most dedicated, vague and yet sharp manner the many ways in which the city is defined by form. With his legendary ambiguity, Rossi believed as much in the permanence of form as in its obsoleteness. These thoughts might resonate more than ever today, in a society where most processes are engaged with the imminent present, when tomorrow is already old-fashioned. Events triggering scenarios easily replace classical urban planning. Processes, behaviors, coordination and any impalpable phenomenon define an ever-aspired flexibility. But meanwhile, architecture acknowledges the past through the simple fact that buildings still should last hundreds of years, in the pure logic of sustainability. Buildings silently assume their permanence, quietly providing shelter to all the great thinkers of ever-changing processes.

We dedicate this issue of CARTHA to the city and to its architecture. Paying tribute to Rossi, we have borrowed the original structure from *The Architecture of the City:* as an empty canvas, to be refilled with a possible contemporary interpretation. Selected authors have each been assigned one of the 33 subtitles of the original book, and were given *carte blanche* to decide in which terms their contribution would directly relate to its precedent and to the topic assigned. The resulting essays and images are as diverse as their authors: artists, architects, writers, and academics, all living in many different parts of the world. This operation was only possible thanks to the fragmentary nature of the original book, itself made up of a collection of essays gathered and loosely composed into an interpretable theory. The rewritten book is as eclectic as its root and, in its very own way, aims at emphasizing the contemporaneity and universality of Rossi's thoughts. Raising questions about authorship, appropriation and interpretation, this many-handed palimpsest intrinsically weaves a city-like structure: a whole without a single author, plots filled by different interpretations of a given rule, many personal ways to appropriate an idea.

 Thus and above all, this issue had the aspiration to be a group work, one that honours the collective *form of form* or "la forme humaine par excellence."

● ① The Structure of Urban Artifacts

● The Individuality of Urban Artifacts
㊝ 56 The Form of the Collective Artifacts
⑵₂₈ Mariabruna Fabrizi
⑵₂₈ Fosco Lucarelli

● The Urban Artifact as a Work of Art
㊝ 58 Le Corbusier's Raised Arm Gestures a backstroke
⑵₃₄ Ala Younis

● Typological Questions
㊝ 60 The Timelessness of Form: An Apocryphal Interview with Aldo Rossi and Christopher Alexander
⑵₃₁ Nelson Mota

● Critique of Naive Functionalism
㊝ 62 No One Wants to Talk about Unicorns
⑵₃₀ Ahmad Makia

● Problems of Classification
㊝ 64 Problems of Classification
⑵₂₈ José Pedro Cortes

● The Complexity of Urban Artifacts ⬤ Madrid, Moneo and the Complexity of Urban Artifacts ⓘ233 Alejandro Valdivieso

● Monuments and the Theory of Permanences ⓘ70 Monuments and the Theory of Permanences ⓘ229 Ganko

● 11 Primary Elements and the Concept of Area

● The Study Area
72 The Study Area
230 Armin Linke

● Residential Districts as Study Areas
76 Zurich as a Case Study
228 Irina Davidovici

● The Individual Dwelling
78 Dwelling
230 Martin Marker Larsen
234 Christian Vennerstrøm Jensen

● The Typological Problem of Housing in Berlin
80 The Typological Problem of Housing in Berlin
233 Something Fantastic

● Garden City and the Ville Radieuse
84 Garden City and the Ville Radieuse
234 Camille Zakharia

● Primary Elements
⑨² John Hejduk's Berlin Tower –
A Shape Called Home
⑵²⁷ Shumon Basar

● The Dynamic of Urban Elements
⑨⁴ The Dynamic of Urban Elements (Stillness under the Moving Eye)
⑵³⁴ Cino Zucchi

● The Ancient City
⑨⁸ The Ancient City
⑵³³ Giovanna Silva

● Processes of Transformation
⑩⁰ Dead Palms
⑵³³ Ursa:
⑵²⁸ Alexandre Delmar
⑵³² Margarida Quintã
⑵³³ Luís Ribeiro da Silva

● Geography and History; the Human Creation
⑩² Notes on Aldo Rossi's Geography and History; the Human Creation
⑵²⁷ Adrià Carbonell
⑵³² Roi Salgueiro Barrio

III. The Individuality of Urban Artifacts, Architecture

- The *Locus*
- 104 The *Locus*
- 229 Stefano Graziani

- Architecture as Science
- 106 Post-Critical Urbanism
- 232 Philippe Rahm

- Urban Ecology and Psychology
- 108 Urban Ecology and Psychology
- 233 Gabriel Tomasulo

- How Urban Elements Become Defined
- 110 Rossi the Ambiguous
- 230 Nicholas Lobo Brennan

- The Roman Forum
- 112 The Roman Forum
- 226 Annette Amberg

- Monuments; Summary of the Critique of the Concept of Context
- 114 The City of Architecture
- 231 Daniele Pisani

● The City as History
116 The City as History, History as Life
231 Nicolò Ornaghi

● The Collective Memory
118 The Collective Memory
230 Walter Mair

● Athens
122 Two Reverse Urban Artifacts in Athens
230 Nikos Magouliotis

● Ⅳ The Evolution of Urban Artifacts

● The City as Field of Application for Various Forces, Economics ⓗ㉖ The City as Field of Application for Various Forces, Economics ㉙㉙ Owen Hatherley

● The Thesis of Maurice Halbwachs ⓗ㉘ The Thesis of Maurice Halbwachs ㉖㉖ Bureau A

● Further Considerations on the Nature of Expropriations ⓗ㉚ Six Buildings on an Island or Planning for the Tropics ㉔㉞ WAI Architecture Think Tank: Cruz Garcia Nathalie Frankowski

● Land Ownership ⓘ㉞ Land Ownership ㉙㉙ Cloé Gattigo

● The Housing Problem ⓘ㉟ The Ordinary in the Problem of Housing ㉗㉗ Laura Bonell ㉗㉗ Daniel López-Dòriga

Territory?
● The Urban Scale
(140) The Architecture of the
(233) Milica Topalovic

● Politics as Choice
(144) Politics as Choice
(226) Pier Vittorio Aureli

The Form of the Collective Artefacts

In the context of the exhibition *The Form of Form,* at the Lisbon Architecture Triennale 2016, three maps of three paradigmatic proto-cities are presented. The black and white plan drawings are stripped of information in order to highlight the bare form of the cities. As apparently abstract as they are, these documents immediately reveal forms that at this stage in history are capable of absorbing and communicating a large set of values connected to the construction of the city and its social organization.

The town of Çatalhöyük, today located in Turkey, the pueblos of Chaco Canyon in New Mexico, and Biskupin in Poland, are three settlements belonging to three different times in history. While differing in their general urban planimetry, the three ancient cities bear several common traits that make them comparable.

First of all, the form of each of these primordial cities is instantly recognizable; second, the urban form is obtained from the continuous agglomeration of a basic, individual artefact: the single cell. This space hosts the bare functions of living, those we could call "domestic," but it also embodies social meaning and ritual purpose; in Çatalhöyük, bodies were buried under the floors, and the walls were painted with vivid, sacred images.

Only in the case of Chaco Canyon are the cells, called the "pit houses," coupled with larger rooms, called "kivas," which apparently hosted collective spaces. Even when these variations are introduced, the assembling rules that govern the whole urban system are repetitive, and those that generate architecture are strictly interdependent with the ones generating the city.

In these proto-cities, architecture does not seem to "express only one aspect of a complex reality," but is still able, at this age in history, to directly embody specific material needs and a clear social structure.

The social organization lying behind the form of the three settlements appears, in fact, to be one based upon a community of equals, where everyone, regardless of gender or age, occupies the same social and physical space. The absence of a class structure implies an absence of formal representation of class differences: the construction of the material and spatial structures constituting the single architectures (walls, roofs, rooms), and the urban artefact as a whole, is in direct response to pure necessity.

The form of the city appears, then, as the result of a purely quantitative addition of domestic modules adapted only to topography and with the added value, especially in the case of Biskupin, of producing a defensive layer.

At this primordial stage, architecture has no individuality and is one thing with the urban form. In the case of Çatalhöyük, the relationship is even more extreme. as the roofs of the houses are used for communal activities, as well as serving as the only connecting infrastructure of the houses. One might say that the house absorbs all urban functions, material and representative, and contains the rules to form (the form of) the city.

At the dawn of civilization, and many ages before functionalism came to be an ideological setting for the construction of architecture and the city, even the most basic distinction of functions associated with specific spaces does not yet exist. The cell is the barest form of what will be the "house," but is already something different from the primitive hut: it not only protects people from weather conditions and outside dangers, but settles the rules for sharing a territory, provides a collective meaning, and structures the form of the city.

Mariabruna Fabrizi
Fosco Lucarelli

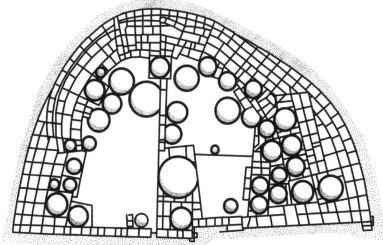

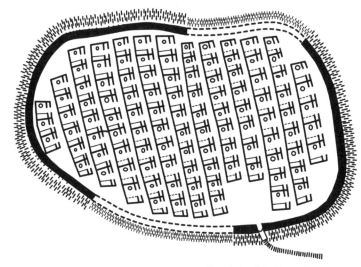

City of Çatalhöyük, southern Anatolia, (approximately 7500 BCE to 5700 BCE)
Settlement of Biskupin, Poland, (approximately 800 BCE)
Pueblo of Chaco Canyon, New Mexico, USA, (approximately 850 to 1250 CE)

Le Corbusier's Raised Arm Gestures a Backstroke

In his first visit to Baghdad in 1957, Le Corbusier asked Iraq's Director of Physical Education: "A swimming pool with waves?" Enthusiasm over a pool with artificial waves was stoked by their mutual interest in aqua sports. What Le Corbusier and the Iraqis wanted for the Sport Center was a structure that would embody a modern Mesopotamia, whose architecture would feature waters channelled from the Tigris and an artificial wave pool collected from its flow. From then on, planning Baghdad became a strategy, an expression of power – or a necessity when it takes the form of enabling a future possibility.

In 1959, the Ministry of Public Works and Housing asked Le Corbusier: "What do you think about the creation of a second stadium in Baghdad?" He answered: "In principle it appears to me to be quite useless, as it minimizes the one or the other by a sterile competition between them."[1]

Le Corbusier's Saddam Hussein Gymnasium metamorphosed through numerous iterations of plans over a period of twenty-five years before it was finally inaugurated in 1980. Up until then, the commission passed through five military coups; six heads of state; four master plans, each with its own town planner; a Development Board that became a Ministry and then a State Commission; a modern starchitect among a constellation of many others with their associated architects, draftsmen, contractors, translators and lawyers; local architects accompanied by similar structures from their own consulting firms, from government departments and parallel commissions; more than one local artist/sculptor; eager competitors; and other monuments that appeared and disappeared as a result of these same conglomerations.

The Baghdad-based consulting firm Iraq Consult (1952–1978), led by its founder Rifat Chadirji (1926–), facilitated the continuously interrupted process of building the gymnasium. In addition to his involvement in other aspects of the project, Chadirji took a set of 35 mm photographs of the Gymnasium in 1982. These photographs and other documents of the urban artefacts he built exist now in the form of montages made up of scraps smuggled in and out of Abu Ghraib prison while Chadirji served part of a life sentence. The architect produced these compilations as he edited his notes into a massive monograph that renders the development of his architectural philosophy within the context of the modernity-identity discourse and his local and international commissions, and how these were affected by political conflict.

In December 2011, I asked the exiled architect about the parallel fates of the Gymnasium and its creators. From his response, it seemed to me that he revisited the enthusiasm that had driven the international architectural endeavors. At 85, he considered that his work in introducing samples of international modernism was only in order for these projects to be experienced first-hand by the students and citizens of Baghdad. In another expression of dismay, he said that his buildings were being demolished one after another.

Chadirji's first statement illustrated an interesting image of power relations in architecutre; to outsource architects to present structures on a platform for local viewers removes any attributed or attempted locality and reduces the buildings to their basic relationship with their makers. The urban artefacts, in this image, become basic forms that aggregate, propagate, and negate forms of other structures. Perhaps this power relation is what Le Corbusier tried to explain when he responded to the question regarding a second stadium, or the fates Chadirji was refusing in his second statement.

Le Corbusier created an image of such power relations in his model of the superstructures for his *Cité radieuse* in Marseille. On an inclined platform, he presented multiple architectural forms existing next to each other; the background was an image, and there were no other structures around nor beneath this presentation. Whether serving the residents of the main structure beneath (the building) or the city, in the images produced by Le Corbusier's model and Chadirji's statement, the

Ala Younis

Plan for Greater Baghdad (2015) by Ala Xounis

buildings are meant to come to the foreground, emptied of all players. Between these forms and a sweeping landscape, two spaces remain: one of pure air permeating between the buildings, and an overall one containing space that surrounds the block of forms interchanging their power, in a secluded universe where nothing else exists.

Plan for Greater Baghdad is a project heavily based on archives, found images and objects that reproduce the story and politics around the Saddam Hussein Gymnasium project in the form of a timeline, an architectural model and a set of characters. The characters reproduce citations of imageless gestures that relate to performances of design, power, and designing power. They are retrieved as a set of motions and signals enacted by characters frozen in the denouements of historical time: Chadirji jogging in the courtyard of Abu Ghraib Prison or hurrying to photograph his monument before it is demolished; a young Saddam Hussein on the edges of the scene as the monuments' (de)constructor; and Le Corbusier raising his arm to gesture the backstroke of an artificial wave in a swimming pool that would pull its waters from the Tigris. On an inclined base, an architectural model of the gymnasium is fixed next to, but different in proportion from, the set of characters. The setup aims to look at monuments, their architects and the governments they worked for. through the alternating power relations between them in the times of shifting states. In the diverse iterations of the project, these elements morph as they migrate within a universe of possible artistic and architectural intentions.

1   Report by Director General, Technical Section 2, Baghdad, titled "Baghdad Stadium, Notes: From Mr. Le Corbusier, Architect," May 4, 1959.

The Timelessness of Form: An Apocryphal Interview with Aldo Rossi and Christopher Alexander

This interview never happened. The answers provided by Aldo Rossi were all collected from the section *Typological Questions* in the first American edition of his *The Architecture of the City,* published in 1982. The answers given by Christopher Alexander were gathered from a chapter in his *The Timeless Way of Building,* published in 1979. In both cases the original spelling was preserved.

>Nelson Mota (NM): The reason for bringing you two together is your common interest in time and temporality as key factors in the rapport between nature and urban artifacts. Aldo calls it the creation of an "artificial homeland" and Christopher names it "the timeless way of building." How far back should we look in order to make sense of this relationship?

Aldo Rossi (AR): The "artificial homeland" is as old as man. Bronze Age men adapted the landscape to social needs by constructing artificial islands of brick, by digging wells, drainage canals, and watercourses. [...] Neolithic villages already offered the first transformations of the world according to man's needs.
Christopher Alexander (CA): [The timeless way of building] is thousands of years old, and the same today as it has always been. The great traditional buildings of the past, the villages and tents and temples in which man feels at home, have always been made by people who were very close to the center of this way.

>NM: Both of you describe the act of building as being fundamentally a social practice. Does this mean, though, that building practices are particular to a specific time and place?

AR: The first forms and types of habitation, as well as temples and more complex buildings, were [...] developed according to both needs and aspirations to beauty; a particular type was associated with a form and a way of life, although its specific shape varied widely from society to society. [...] I would define the concept of type as something that is permanent and complex, a logical principle that is prior to form and that constitutes it.
CA: At the core of all successful acts of building and at the core of all successful processes of growth, even though there are a million different versions of these acts and processes, there is one fundamental invariant feature, which is responsible for their success. Although this way has taken on a thousand different forms at different times, in different places, still, there is an unavoidable, invariant core to all of them.

>NM: You both highlighted permanence or invariance as a key feature in successful acts of building. Can these acts still be copied or replicated in this day and age?

CA: There is a definable sequence of activities which are at the heart of all acts of building, and it is possible to specify, precisely, under what conditions these activities will generate a building which is alive. All this can be made so explicit that anyone can do it.

>NM: Could you clarify what that sequence of activities is, Christopher? Have you discovered a sort of formula that everybody can use to create great buildings?

CA: This one way of building has always existed. [...] In an unconscious form, this way has been behind almost all ways of building for thousands of years. [...] But it has become possible to identify it only now, by going to a level of analysis which is deep enough to show what is invariant in all the different versions of this way.

> NM: Aldo, do you agree with Christopher on the idea that there is a sort of inherent rule that performs as a structuring principle of architecture, and that we should be able to identify?

AR: In fact, it can be said that this principle is a constant. Such an argument presupposes that the architectural artifact is conceived as a structure and that this structure is revealed and can be recognized in the artifact itself. As a constant, this principle, which we can call the typical element, or simply the type, is to be found in all architectural artifacts. It is also then a cultural element, and as such can be investigated in different architectural artifacts; typology becomes, in this way, the analytical moment of architecture, and it becomes readily identifiable at the level of urban artifacts.

> NM: Does this mean that we can glean information on how to build a housing complex today from, for example, a Roman insula?

AR: I tend to believe that housing types have not changed from antiquity up to today, but this is not to say that the actual way of living has not changed, nor that new ways of living are not always possible. The house with a loggia is an old scheme; a corridor that gives access to rooms is necessary in plan and present in any number of urban houses. But there are a great many variations on this theme among individual houses at different times.
CA: The power to make buildings beautiful lies in each of us already. It is a core so simple, and so deep, that we are born with it.

> NM. Do you mean that metaphorically?

CA: This is no metaphor. I mean it literally. Imagine the greatest possible beauty and harmony in the world – the most beautiful place that you have ever seen or dreamt of. You have the power to create it, at this very moment, just as you are.

> NM: Could you clarify that? How do I have that power? How do architects have that power? What do we need to activate it?

CA: To become free of all these artificial images of order which distort the nature that is in us, we must first learn a discipline which teaches us the true relationship between ourselves and our surroundings. Then, once this discipline has done its work, and pricked the bubbles of illusion which we cling to now, we will be ready to give up the discipline and act as nature does. This is the timeless way of building: learning the discipline – and shedding it.

> NM: Aldo, do you think that typological studies can help us in "pricking the bubbles of illusion," as Christopher puts it, which are created by dogmatic architectural systems, codes or methods?

AR: Ultimately, we can say that type is the very idea of architecture, that which is closest to its essence. In spite of changes, it has always imposed itself on the "feelings and reason" as the principle of architecture and of the city. [...] Typology is an element that plays its own role in constituting form; it is a constant. The problem is to discern the modalities within which it operates and, moreover, its effective value.

No One Wants to Talk about Unicorns[1]

In the fall of last year, Eric Yearwood, a stand-up comedian and actor, was asked to perform for a film project that was meant to create viral internet content. In the film, Eric will pretend to be asleep at a New York subway platform. Eric will be carrying a phone. While asleep, a rat will crawl onto him. The rat will access his phone, launch the camera option and click the photo icon to capture a self-portrait, or selfie. Afterwards, Eric will leap up and act surprised.

Eric's co-star, the sophisticated, acquiescent rat, is a recruit of Zardulu, the scriptwriter and producer of the film project. This rat is one of the many professionally trained rodents from Zardulu's studio-gymnasium, in which they "would run [around a] maze[...], leap over little obstacles ... there was ... a little pool that they would swim across to retrieve certain things. And she had them trained in a way that was pretty amazing."[2] For the video project featuring Eric, Zardulu will smear the phone's "Home" button with peanut butter, tricking the rat into taking a picture. The film is part of Zardulu's extensive body of work, comprised of coordinated, deliberate illusions and absurdities across New York City. In Eric's testimony, he explains how Zardulu's studio is filled with creations, such as a suit of human hair, made specifically for spreading fantastical tales across the world.

Eric, naturally, accepted the opportunity without much hesitation. (He was compensated for his efforts, too.) A few days after completing the shoot, Zardulu submits the video to Connecticut TV, posing as Don Richards. The video goes viral and today is commemorated as the magical phenomenon of "Selfie Rat." Soon after, different media platforms pick up the story and comments begin to pour in as analysts, eyewitnesses and professional debunkers alike all have their say. This, coupled with the older news of "Pizza Rat", where a rat is filmed transporting a slice of pizza through New York's subway system, created a very small trend in our contemporary media where rats were portrayed as extraterrestrial, hyper-urbanized creatures. These works by Zardulu, moreover, circulate and compile content for varying landscapes: topographical – relying on physical witnesses – as well as digital, tailored for the clickbait industry.

Suddenly, a member of the public identifies Eric in the video as an actor, and the Selfie Rat hoax is exposed on the internet. Pizza Rat's authenticity comes into question, too, as another possible video manipulation. Covertly, a public discourse emerges about what is real and what is not. Eric promised to maintain anonymity regarding this project, but after the hoax scandal he spoke out for Zardulu. Zardulu did the same by establishing Twitter and Facebook accounts. On those platforms, she described herself as a performance artist whose purpose is to reinvent the lost and undervalued practices of mythmaking. Thus, both performers, through their testimonies, made possible the idea that many of the absurd things seen in New York's subway system could be Zardulu's preternatural machinations that perform along with the daily rhythms of the city. A few weeks later, another person reports two rats coordinating the transfer of a slice of pita bread up the subway stairs. Only if you spiral down the illusionary world of Zardulu can you begin to understand how effective it is. The narrative that emerges is a hysteria spreading across the world, where people are negotiating the possibility that rats and their operations were coordinated by a mythic figure, who goes by the fictional name Zardulu, in a metropolitan and gridded city such as New York. To achieve this in the age of ever-densifying biopolitical governmental intelligence is a victory.

The project's ultimate success, moreover, is verisimilitude, in which the city's everyday surfaces are brought into being: being of otherworldliness. The medium of Zardulu's work is the terrain of the city, where its matter and inhabitants are not used as illustrations for universal rationality, logic, lineage, structure, grids, history, memories, inheritances and values, but as a force field of combustive and imaginative processes.

 Ahmad Makia

1   This piece is informed by Gimlet Media, Episode 56, Zardulu podcast, released on February 25, 2016.
2   See podcast transcript.

Problems of Classification

228 José Pedro Cortes

VFXira, 2016

Madrid, Moneo and the Complexity of Urban Artifacts

Rafael Moneo (born in Tudela, Navarra, 1937) has lived and works in Madrid since 1954, when he moved from the small city in the north of Spain where he spent his childhood and early youth to begin his university education. Since then, short time periods have suspended his attachment to Madrid, a city that becomes crucial when one begins to investigate Moneo's body of work. After qualifying as an architect in 1961, Moneo moved to Hellebaek in Denmark to work for Jørn Utzon. He returned to Madrid a year later for a short stay before moving to Rome, where he spent two years at the Spanish Academy, a willful period to reflect upon theory and history and the place where he would establish his first linkages with the Italian scenario. In Rome he met Manfredo Tafuri, Paolo Portoghesi, Bruno Zevi[1] and Rudolf Wittkower, amongst other Italian architects and historians. It was not until 1967, back in Spain, where he met Aldo Rossi for the first time, in one of the encounters organized by members of the Schools of Barcelona and Madrid, called the *Pequeños Congresos* (small conferences).

Rossi's *The Architecture of the City* was immediately translated into Spanish and published by the Barcelona-based editorial and publishing house Gustavo Gili in 1971.[2] Architect and professor Salvador Tarragó translated the book[3] and promoted at once the "Rossian" magazine *2C Arquitectura de la Ciudad*,[4] publishing three issues on Rossi. Other publications from Barcelona played an important role as printed spaces committed to the endeavour of disseminating architectural theory, transforming their previous condition as mere descriptive elements of a more and more confusing urban reality, into spaces where this reality was discussed for transformation. They became vehicles through which a new consideration of the city as a collective space of action would be conceived, engaging with Rossi's main statement on cosidering the city – and every urban artefact – to be, by its very nature, collective.

Moneo wrote a paper on Rossi for *2C* in one of the aforementioned monographs.[5] *2C* was contemporaneous with another magazine published in Barcelona during the late 70s, *Arquitecturas Bis, información gráfica de actualidad*[6] of which Moneo was one of the founding members. One of the first pieces Moneo wrote for *AB* was an essay on Rossi and Vittorio Gregotti,[7] which introduced a larger investigation of the former's work, including a discussion of the principles Rossi made explicit in his book. *AB* stood out from other magazines published in Spain, partly due to its connections with several North American and Italian publications, such as *Oppositions* from New York and the Milanese *Lotus.* They practiced an "after-modern" philosophical and historical self-consciousness that contributed to a breaking with the traditions of modernism: theory was understood as a form of practice in its own right. The publication in *Oppositions* of "Aldo Rossi: The Idea of Architecture and the Modena Cemetery"[8] translated Rossi's ideology, and what was known as "architettura autonomia,"[9], to the North American intellectual environment. In 1985, when the last issue of AB was published, Moneo was already working as Chairman of the Department of Architecture at Harvard University, and his role as active translator of Rossi's ideas into North American academia was by then firmly established.

On his return to Spain, between 1991 and 1992,[10], Moneo was working on two projects in Madrid: the new Atocha Station[11] and the Thyssen-Bornemisza Museum.[12] Both are purposefully and carefully redrawn in the city plan, together with the Bank of Spain[13] and the Prado Museum extensions.[14] Atocha, which has recently been extended again according to Moneo's design, has turned out to be the architecture capable of synthesising most accurately Moneo's approach to what Rossi described as "the complexity of urban artefacts." Its design strategy is the assertion of the concept of the city as a totality. The aim was to confer consistency, order and continuity to an urban complex comprising several different parts: the old station, with the preservation of its late nineteenth-century marquee; a new car park area just above the new suburban station; the intercity station, built around and defined according

Alejandro Valdivieso

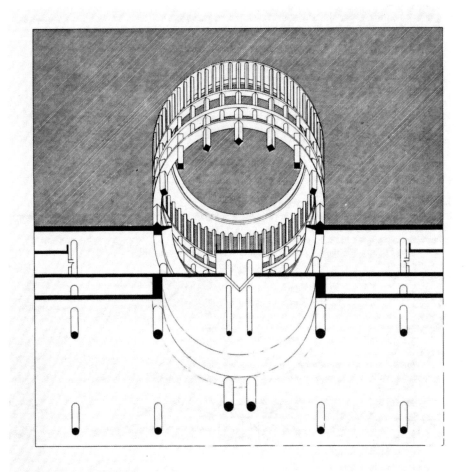

Atocha's intermodal transportation hub: upward isometric projection, using the convention of Auguste Choisy. The drawing portrays the development of the structure, emphasizing both formal attributes and methods of construction. (Rafael Moneo, "Estación de cercanías e intercambiador de Atocha." *Arquitectura,* n°. 255. Madrid: Colegio Oficial de Arquitectos de Madrid, 1985, p. 62).

to the original alignment of tracks; and the intermodal transportation hub that manifests itself as the centerpiece of the architecture resolving Atocha's complexity, as stated by Moneo.[15] The hub reveals itself as a primary element, a permanent structure that ties together the complexity of all the overlapping layouts, movements and directions, but which above all determines and shapes the city. It also unveils what Rossi would describe as the contrast between private and universal, individual and collective, and emerges, like a metaphysical piece inside a painting by de Chirico, as a monument defined by Rossi standing within the landscape of Madrid. Moneo, as constructor of the city whose main intellectual vehicle is history – understood as the accumulation of human experience over time – was concerned with the notion of continuity and permanence, assuming that the city, as Rossi emphasized, endures through its transformations.

1   Moneo translated Bruno Zevi's 1964 edition of Architecture in Nuce [Architettura in nuce] into Spanish. ZEVI, Bruno (1969) *Arquitectura in Nuce. Una definición de arquitectura.* Madrid: Aguilar.
2   Unlike in the United States, where the book was published more than a decade later: ROSSI, Aldo (1982). *The Architecture of the City.* Translation by Diane Ghirardo and Joan Ockman and Introduction by Peter Eisenman; revised for the American edition by Aldo Rossi and Peter Eisenman. Cambridge, Mass.: MIT Press.
3   ROSSI, Aldo (1971). *La arquitectura de la ciudad.* Translation by Josep María Ferrer-Ferrer and Salvador Tarragó Cid. Colección "Arquitectura y Crítica." Barcelona: Gustavo Gili.
4   *2C Construcción de la Ciudad* published a total of 22 issues from 1972 to 1985. Directed by Salvador Tarragó and Carlos Martí Arís.
5   MONEO, Rafael (1979). "La obra reciente de Aldo Rossi: dos reflexiones." *2C Construcción de la Ciudad* No. 14. December 1979. Barcelona: Coop. Ind. De trabajo Asociado "Grupo 2C" S.C.I. Pages 38–39.
6   *Arquitecturas Bis: información gráfica de actualidad* was published in Barcelona from 1974 to 1985, editing a total of 52 issues.

The magazine employed a very efficient intern structure that actively participated in the production and edition of all the numbers, generating around 500 writings; about 30 % of the total content (news notes, theoretical and criticism writings, texts and book reviews). Under the direction of the well-known publisher Rosa Regás, the editorial board was mainly made up of architects and professors – Oriol Bohigas, Federico Correa, Manuel de Solà-Morales, Rafael Moneo, Lluís Domènech, Helio Piñón, and Luis Peña Ganchegui (the latter a member since the 17–18 double issue published in July and September of 1977) – as well as the philosopher Tomás Lloréns and the graphic designer Enric Satué. In 1977, the architect Fernando Villavecchia joined as the Editorial Board secretary.

7 MONEO, Rafael (1974). "Rossi & Gregotti." *Arquitecturas* Bis No. 4 (November 1974). Barcelona: La Gaya Ciencia.

8 "These notes, written in 1973 before the Triennale of 1974, do not deal with the complex notions which provoked that exhibition; with the grouping under the banner of the 'Tendenza' – a heterogeneous, yet consciously selected, group of architects from different countries. Thus these notes are limited to the discussion of Rossi's principles made explicit in his book L´Architettura della Città, and in this light, to see how Rossi designed the Modena Cemetery without considering the propositions inherent in the Triennale even though Rossi was undoubtedly the inspiration for these ideas." MONEO, Rafael (1976). Aldo Rossi: "The Idea of Architecture and the Modena Cemetery." *Oppositions* No. 5. *A Journal for Ideas and Criticism in Architecture.* Summer 1976. New York: Institute for Architecture and Urban Studies. [Original: MONEO, Rafael (1974) "La idea de Arquitectura en Rossi y el Cementerio de Modena." Barcelona: Ediciones de la ETSAB].

9 [...] "Moneo makes the connection between the two aspects inherent in Rossi's work by breaking the article into two dialectic halves: each with its own theme and its own rhythm and cadence. The first part, which dissects Rossi's thinking in his book *The Architecture of the City*, is more intense; the second part, which examines Rossi's project for the Modena cemetery, is more lyrical. For me, this is architecture writing at its best – dense and informative, analytical and questioning. There is no question that Rossi's metaphysics demand this kind of dissection. Equally important for the European context is the fact that such an article by Moneo, who was part of the Barcelona group of writers of the magazine *Arquitecturas Bis,* signals a possible change in the Milan/Barcelona axis: from the influence in the early sixties of Vittorio Gregotti and post-war functionalism to the new ideology present in Rossi's work" [...]. EISENMAN, Peter (1976) Prologue to Moneo's text "The Idea of Architecture and the Modena Cemetery." ibid.

10 During his professorship at the School of Barcelona, Moneo continue living and working in Madrid, commuting to Barcelona to teach every week. During this time he developed two important works: the Bankinter Building in Madrid (1972–76) and the Logroño town hall (1973–81). During his years at Harvard, as Chair of the Department of Architecture from 1985 to 1990, Moneo moved to Cambridge, Massachusetts, with his family, and although he opened a small office in Massachusetts Avenue, near Harvard Square, the main office remained in Madrid.

11 Atocha Station extension, Madrid (1984–92). In collaboration with Emilio Tuñón. First prize winner in competition (1983). Phase I (1985–88): Suburban station and intermodal transportation hub. Phase II (1988–92): Intercity station and nineteenth-century marquee building (architect Alberto Del Palacio, 1894). Phase III (2008–2010): Extension of the intercity station. Renovation of the Palace of Villahermosa: Museum Thyssen-Bornemisza, Madrid. 1989–1992.Bank of Spain extension (competition winner, 1978–80, built in 2004–06).Prado Museum extension (first prize in competition 1998, 1998–2007).

12 MONEO, Rafael (2010). *El Croquis* Nos. 20+64+98: *Rafael Moneo: imperative anthology, 1967–2004.* El Escorial, Madrid: El Croquis Editorial, p. 206–223.

13 Bank of Spain extension (competition winner, 1978–80, built in 2004–06).

14 Prado Museum extension (first prize in competition 1998, 1998–07).

15 MONEO, Rafael (2010). *El Croquis* n.20+64+98: *Rafael Moneo: Imperative Anthology, 1967–2004.* El Escorial, Madrid: El Croquis Editorial, p. 206–223.

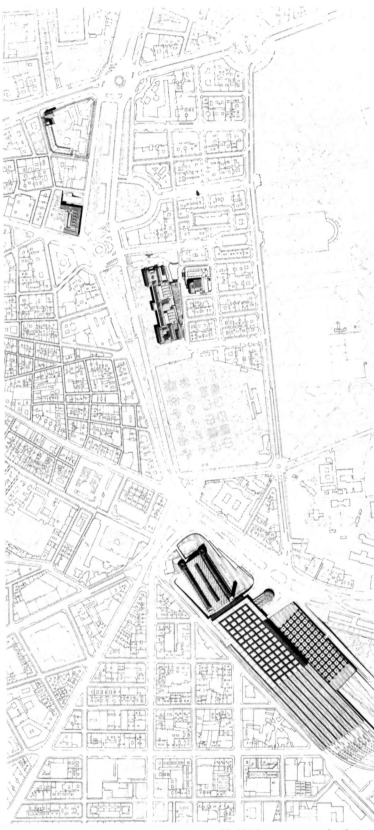

Madrid downtown area plan that includes the Bank of Spain and the Prado Museum extensions, the Thyssen-Bornemisza Museum and Atocha Railway Station (Rafael Moneo, *Remarks on 21 works*. New York: Monacelli Press, 2010, p. 168).

Monuments and the Theory of Permanences

There is nothing new in all of this. Yet in attempting to formulate a
theory of urban artifacts that is consistent with reality, I have benefited
from highly diverse sources.

"Monuments and the Theory of Permanence" concludes the first chapter of The Architecture of The City. Among the four chapters of the book, this is the only one in which Rossi succeeds in restraining the centrifugal tendencies of its discourse. By virtue of a great effort of synthesis, here, Rossi achieves important results.

With "Monuments and the Theory of Permanence" a particular idea of the city's place in relation to the ordinance of time reaches its ultimate formulation. This idea sets-up the (unfulfilled) premise for a theory of the city where new and old parts – suburbs and town centers, mediocrity and monumentality – become part of a progressive and unitary plan embracing "all" of the contemporary city.

With "Monuments and the Theory of Permanence", Rossi takes distances himself from the simplifications of both modern utopias and postmodern nostalgias in order to explore the complexity of the contemporary city; its technical advancements as well as the memory deposited in it throughout history.

With "Monuments and the Theory of Permanence" – in accordance to what Rossi calls: "consistency with reality" – both past and future per se are rejected as moments detached from the concrete experience of life. Yet, for the sake of a deeper understanding of the present, the past may prove of particular interest.

> One must remember that the difference between past and future [...]
> in large measure reflects the fact that the past is partly being experienced
> now, and this may be the meaning to give permanences: they are
> a past that we are still experiencing.

At the very same time, to the extent that it exerts passive resistance towards new forms of appropriation, the past (i.e, the monumental structure of the city) is felt by Rossi as the equivalent of a pathological condition: an obstacle to the pursuit of one's duties and pleasures.

> In this respect, permanences present two aspects: on the one hand,
> they can be considered as propelling elements; on the other, as pathological
> elements.

Rossi's position regarding the time of the city is problematic:

> The form of the city is always the form of a particular time of the city;
> but there are many times in the formulation of the city, and a city may change
> its face even in the course of one's man life, its original references ceasing
> to exist.

However, a comparison with traditional views can enlighten Rossi's stance. "Earlier urban thinking had placed the modern city in phased history: between a benighted past and a rosy future (the Enlightenment view) or as a betrayal of a golden past (the Romantic view)." According to Rossi "[...] by contrast, the city [has] no structured temporal locus between past and future, but rather a temporal quality. The modern city offer[s] an eternal hic et nunc, whose content [is] transience, but whose transience [is] permanent. The city present[s] a succession of variegated, fleeting moments, each to be savoured in its passage from nonexistence to oblivion."[1] According to Rossi, the present is not simply the point of transition between past and future, but rather the point of convergence of multiple pasts and possible futures. Therefore, it cannot be judged in terms of "progress" or "decadence." In this context, monuments play a particular role, as the formal infrastructure allowing for the permanence, as well as the sudden reappearance of a collective sacred memory within the otherwise profane character of modern civilization. Suspended in a state of eternal present, according to Rossi, monuments mediate between permanence and change, past and future, playing both a conservative and a propelling role.

> I mainly want to establish [...] that the dynamic process of the city tends more to evolution than preservation, and that in evolution monuments are not only preserved but continuously presented as propelling elements of development.

Rossi's theory of permanence brings together two conflicting concepts of the city's evolution. A positive idea of the city as progress inherited from authors like Voltaire, Fichte and Mumford – the city as the culture-forming agent par excellence; the site as well as the symbol of civilization – is blended with the fatalism of a concept of the city as *destiny* – the city as "[...] a collective fatality which could know only personal solutions, not social ones."[2] – influenced by the *kulturpessimismus* of Burckhardt, Spengler and Beaudelaire.

As distantly as it is affected by both utopia and nostalgia, the ambiguous stance toward one's own time outlined by "Monuments and the Theory of Permanence" is a difficult whole seeking a tricky reconciliation of opposites. Nevertheless, Rossi's idea of "consistency with reality" is not only the main achievement of *The Architecture of the City.* Also, it is still a realistic work hypothesis.

1   Schorske, E. Carl, "The Idea of the City in European Thought: Voltaire to Spengler," in Burchard, John E., Handlin, Oscar, eds., *The Historian and the City,* Cambridge, Mass., 1963, p. 109. In the original text Schorske is referring to Charles Beaudelaire. The French poet is a fundamental reference for Rossi's theory and is explicitly quoted at the end of the paragraph.
2   Schorske, E. Carl, p.111. In this case, Schorske is referring to the conception of the city by the Austrian poet Rainer Maria Rilke.

72 II The Study Area

Armin Linke

Mexico City, Mexico, 1999

Mountain with antennas,
Kitakyushu, Japan, 2016

Zurich as a Case Study

In Rossi's studio at ETH Zurich between 1972 and 1974, students were asked to produce detailed surveys of the city's central districts. The analysis of the historical urban fabric in its existing form was part of a design methodology based on typology, which he cultivated as a practical application of *Architettura della Città.* Based on the premise that the chapter "Residential Districts as Study Areas" was a theoretical precursor to Rossi's ETH semesters, it is possible to review the Zurich of today in relation to Rossi's 1966 text.

Seen conceptually, Zurich's ascendance to a global status is consistent with a pattern correlating political events, physical changes in the urban fabric, and population growth. Throughout its history, the city was animated by an impulse towards centrifugal expansion. In the sixteenth century, the militant effort to impose the Reformed faith on other cantons rendered Zurich the center of Protestant Switzerland, lending it a Europe-wide significance. In the nineteenth century, its drive for political reform and modernization led to Zurich hosting two important federal institutions, the Polytechnikum and the first section of the railways, both programmatic elements for the creation of a unified, modern Switzerland. In 1855, the same year the Polytechnikum was founded, the medieval walls were torn down, initiating a long-term trend of urban expansion. Nineteen outlying municipalities were politically incorporated in a first stage in 1893 and a second one in 1934, practically doubling the size of the city. At the same time, the population increased greatly with industrialization and the creation of large factory quarters, both along the railways and to the north and west of the main city.

This process of urban growth underlines the creation of what Rossi calls "residential districts:" characterful, relatively small areas, clearly distinct from each other yet stitched together into an urban collage. Zurich's heterogeneity provides an excellent illustration of the Rossian city as "a system" of "relatively autonomous parts", "each with its own characteristics."[1] In Zurich, these "parts," each with its own personality, are at the same time familiar equivalents of pan-European urban tableaux. The narrow, winding medieval streets of the historical core, the palatial grandeur of the tiny old banking district, the working-class housing colonies of Red Zurich, 1930s stone-clad rationalist institutions and 1950s residential towers appear like conceptual miniatures of European urban episodes. Like a precursor of Rossi's later *Città analoga* collage, Zurich thus becomes a cabinet of urban fragments, each with its raison d'être and own limited order.

Since the city is so small, the various cityscapes occur in restricted territories, sometimes only a few hundred meters long and a couple of streets wide. Characteristically of Zurich, the borders between these districts, be they natural or man-made, are prominent and final. The natural constraints that first defined the settlement, two low mountain ranges and the glacial lake between, have continued to shape its development leading to a paradoxical, "bipolar" growth. When natives refer to the split structure of their city, they perceive a rift between one unit formed by the historical center and its immediately adjacent quartiers, and another comprising industrial and postindustrial growth to the west and the north. The northern expansion towards Schwamendingen, the Oerlikon industrial district and Kloten Airport is interrupted by the artificial rural idyll of Zürichberg, a carefully untouched, forested hill overlooking the city. Its introverted culture of exclusive villas, little isolated farmyards and luxury hotels is replicated by the smaller settlements stringing southwards along the shores of Lake Zurich. Together they signal the formation of a "clear topography of prosperity" centered around central Zurich and extending to the so-called *Goldküste* along the sunny side of the lake.[2]

Zurich's division along the central and northern development nodes does not presuppose that either is a unity. The center is profoundly divided, sliced three ways by the river Limmat, its confluence with the river Sihl, and the wide stretch of railway that cuts across the western side of the city. In its dimensions and decisiveness, the presence of this transport infrastructure is equivalent to that of a third river in the way it cuts across the industrial city fabric. In contrast to the tendency of great European cities to conceal the railways beneath raised parapets and under ground, here they are on display, structuring the urban fabric and influencing the way people move through the city. The new apartment and office towers built along this stretch are oriented towards a panoramic view grounded by a field of steel rails, its horizon underlined by parallel cables and passing trains.

The character of the medieval centre and that of the nineteenth-century bourgeois and industrial residential districts and the contrast between modernist insertions and the gentrified old factory quarters attest to the fact that Zurich's heterogeneity is not the effect of simple functional zoning. Rossi's reading helps us understand that Zurich is an assembly of "morphological and structural units, [each] characterized by a certain urban landscape, a certain social content, and its function."[3] Its characteristic heterogeneity is the prerogative of residential districts as "complex urban artifacts," densely grouped together yet abruptly separated into distinct units of collective meaning.

1   Aldo Rossi, *The Architecture of the City,* 1966, p. 65.
2   Roger Diener, Jacques Herzog, Marcel Meili, Pierre de Meuron, Christian Schmid. Studio Basel, Switzerland: *An Urban Portrait,* Birkhäuser 2006, 618–620.
3   Aldo Rossi, *The Architecture of the City*, 1966, p. 65.

Dwelling

The following are simple thoughts, images and a bit of text that have been traveling between Switzerland and Bahrain in the summer of 2016. The starting point, was a series of images capturing the simple fact that over the last 40–50 years, the town of A'ali has grown in size and density expanding into the ancient burial fields of Bahrain. Many thousands of single-person or family-sized mounds have been cleared to make space for new infrastructure and housing. Several mounds have been significantly altered to make space for private parking and roads. Some grave chambers have been exposed to the city, while others have been halfway dissected, leaving only a few cuts open and the remaining mound intact. The static mounds have become part of a dynamic web of relations and interrelations that flow within a contemporary city. This cohabitation affects not only the city, but also these structures. The result is an interesting relationship between something as dynamic as life and something as static as death.

By being part of the city, these burial places become part of the collective unconsciousness. Like churches or monasteries, they are simple signs, static urban facts – and yet they are undeniably part of the everyday life surrounding them. Maybe the contemporary life needs these stable points to establish a relationship to death. But why should a permanent place be important to the dead when the living that keep their memories alive are constantly moving around in a non-permanent way. Everything is now mobile and negotiable. Even death is now fluid and dissolvable.

>We keep making piles into cities.
>Cities become piles upon piles.
>And cities become new cities.
>New cities upon old piles.
>We make cities from piles upon dead bodies.
>
>New houses are built around the body.
>Around the body and the needs of the body.
>For practical reasons or for the reason of no practical reason.
>New houses become old houses.
>Keys, nameplates and addresses change hands as cities are smouldering.
>
>And cities are smouldering
>back into piles upon bodies.
>Letting go of being like old skin falling.
>When all has settled
> and the air is clear
>stands a new in its place
>seemingly alike.
>
>The form of
>graves and faith,
>heavy and stable,
>make beds and cover.
>It vibrates inside time and falls apart.
>In unexpected frequencies
>it all falls into piles.

The question is whether our perception of signs is ready to change with the same speed and dynamics as everything surrounding us.

Martin Marker Larsen
Christian Vennerstrøm Jensen

II The Typological Problem of Housing in Berlin

233 Something Fantastic

The type is not the problem, but the material.

Anyway, we enjoy the view from our bed, 200 meters from Alexanderplatz, where a *clematis* creeps over the apple trees, keeping our view on the three old and three young linden trees, between which you could see the TV tower in winter.

84 II Garden City and the Ville Radieuse

Buquwah, 2013

Janussan, 2013

Amwaj Island, 2013

Janabiyah, 2013

ID# John Hejduk's Berlin Tower – A Shape Called Home

I've been living in a special slice of building made from squares, cylinders, rectangles and triangles. These shapes can be childlike or Platonic, abstract or figurative. For the architect John Hejduk, they are probably all of these.

Hejduk will be well known to those within the architectural field but not to those outside it. He built very little in his lifetime: not because he couldn't, but rather, because he chose not to. Instead, he made scratchy drawings of carnivalesque objects wandering Europe. His work constituted a diaspora of subjects and objects. A cast list of melancholia. He wrote many, many poems. He constructed strange installations – also comprised of collages of primary shapes but wrought into animistic life.

He taught, lots. In fact, he said, "I don't make any separations. A poem is a poem. A building's a building. Architecture's architecture. Music is music. I mean, it's all structure. It's structure." And yet I find myself residing in a tower where separation is apparent. I've been residing on the 10th and 11th floors of a former social housing block in Berlin that he architected, where separation is apparent: each room exists in its own independent tower, linked to each other by short, punctuated walkways. The gaps are vantage points from which the city enters the building, or you embody the city.

Again, AND, not OR. The apartment oscillates between spaces that seem "too big" and "too small." It reminds us we only become conscious of space when it is either too big (a cathedral, a palace) or is too small (a railway cabin, a prison cell). For most of us, lived space happens in the middle ground and, as such, washes over us quietly. But not here. There are only seven apartments in total in the building. Fourteen floors. It's utterly irrational – no other developer would condone it – and therefore utterly compelling.

Commissioned by the IBA (Internationale Bauausstellung Berlin) initiative, and finished in 1988, a year before the (nearby) Berlin Wall came down, this piece of pure auteurship stands alone, apart, even from itself. Metallic stars protrude from the outer walls, silently and regularly arrayed. Why? The most convincing story I've heard is that: "They're grips for angels to hold onto when they climb the sides of the tower." (Hejduk was a scholar of angelology.)

Every day when I wake up inside this piece of literature masquerading as architecture, a spectral pulse runs through me. This has been home. I have been a character, another primary form amongst others, visible and invisible. Life here is enchanting and unnerving. It is the force of incisive simplicity, the crisp composition of singular ideas.

Shumon Basar

The Dynamic of Urban Elements (Stillness under the Moving Eye)

Cities stand. Their stones stand up; they remain still, obeying the laws of statics. What is then moving? Their inhabitants running around undertaking their daily activities, the flags flapping on their poles, the clouds casting shadows on their moldings and cobblestones.

A bowl contains soup, but it is made of a different material from its content. Its shape is apt to support a dense liquid and hold its heat for a certain time, but it obviously survives beyond this particular lifespan; and it could be used for very different goals from the ones it was planned for.

The famous quote by Winston Churchill "we shape our buildings, thereafter our buildings shape us," can be applied to bowls and cities as well, in a sort of mirror-image version of the other famous motto, "from the spoon to the city." If the latter states that the form of human artefacts is the result of a unified work style of a supposedly "modern" designer, the former casts light on how much people's lives and behaviors are invisibly guided by the spaces in which they take place.

Are we molluscs custom-producing our own homes or are we rather hermit crabs, looking for an empty shell to host our soft bodies, and migrating from one to another when the previous one is not fit for that purpose any more?

On the two sides of the Atlantic Ocean, and from two very different points of view, in the sixth decade of the last century, two different people discovered – or rather rediscovered – the "stillness" of the city, and in a way also the autonomous character of its elements: Aldo Rossi and Kevin Lynch.

Akin to a moment in a game of musical statues or a freeze-frame video-clip effect, their written and illustrated pictures created a snapshot of the material part of the city. Or better, they froze only some of its elements, specifically those that could appear in the memories and the minds of more than one of its inhabitants. If remembrance is a subjective power, they attributed this privileged state only to things and images that appeared in collective mental maps.

Both Lynch and Rossi understood that this condition of permanence of the physical body of the city was a shared need. It somehow coincided with the notion of "habit," of convention, of custom, and more generally with the public realm. Stillness is what founded the city as a public artefact, and prevented its spaces from being the mere result of the Brownian movement of its occupants and vehicles.

In the planning and urban design of the sixties and seventies, urban form was typically seen as the final output of a process where a series of data and inputs had to be enhanced via the means of the "black box" of a planning or design "method."[1] Following this attitude, the issue of form had no real consistence, since in the end it was just the solidification of a functional diagram: Walter Gropius's speech at the Brussels Congrès International d'Architecture Moderne (CIAM) in 1930 on the dilemma of whether to build "Low, Mid- or High-Rise Buildings?" advocated the latter of the three solutions, on the grounds of increased sun exposure and building economy issues.[2]

If the Italian word *monumento* refers explicitly to the role of a building as a reminder of a historical event or of a powerful ruler, the English word "landmark" overlooks issues of content and emphasizes instead its mere physical relevance. According to Wikipedia, it is "a recognisable natural or artificial feature used for navigation, a feature that stands out from its near environment and is often visible from long distances." The contemporary meaning of this word is therefore very close to what Rem Koolhaas defines as "Automonument."[3]

The wanderings Boston pedestrians in Lynch's *The Image of the City* (1960) or the four-wheeled amniotic sacs in his *The View from the Road* (1965) need landmarks to orient themselves in the flux of the metropolis; be they grain elevators (already represented as monuments by Le Corbusier *in Toward an Architecture* (1923), the dome of Washington's Capitol (not so dissimilar from the one that Albert Speer designed for Hitler to complete Berlin's grand axis; often the architectures of political opposite systems are disturbingly similar) or a sketch of the 1939 New York World's Fair Trylon and Perisphere structures, they represent the necessitated visual pointers in the extended geography of the new territory.

If cars flow around the fixity of the "monument/automonument/landmark" in Lynch's continuous "space," little armies of masons and carpenters climb on them in Aldo Rossi's seamless "time." His conception of the monument is a lively one, as its "autonomous" form – whose founding elements are typological simplicity, significant mass and formal clarity rather than stylistic issues – seems to ignite in successive generations of urbanites realizations of unexpected potentials. The original title of Aldo Rossi's chapter is actually *Tensione degli elementi urbani,* where "tension" is still a term belonging to the discipline of statics before the one of dynamics.

Rossi's monuments are peculiar points in the urban structure, enduring in their "final" incarnation while at the same time endlessly reworked over, like the never-ending story of the Fabbrica del Duomo in Milan or the plans by Pope Sixtus V to convert the Colosseum into a housing block containing a wool mill.

The monument is still, yet the monument also stirs the dynamics of urban mutation, and focuses attention on the patterns of the open public spaces around it. It is a clear and simple concept; but as with other "necessary" ones, it re-emerges periodically from the sea of intellect like a wandering whale.

In fact, the dialectic between the structured body of the monument and the flowing paths of its visual and cognitive perception was masterfully expressed seventy years before the first edition of Rossi's *The Architecture of the City,* by a twenty-three year old writer who was asked by the magazine *La Nouvelle Revue* to write something about the work of Leonardo da Vinci. Although puzzled by his output, they had the courage to publish his astounding "self-fulfilling prophecy:"

> The monument (which composes the City which in turn is almost the whole
> of civilization) is such a complex entity that our understanding of
> it passes through several successive phases. First we grasp a changeable
> background that merges with the sky, then a rich texture of motifs in
> height, breadth and depth, infinitely varied by perspective, then something
> solid, bold, resistant, with certain animal characteristics – organs,
> members – then finally a machine having gravity for its motive force, one
> that carries us in thought from geometry to dynamics and thence to the most
> tenuous speculations of molecular physics, suggesting as it does not
> only the theories of that science but the models used to represent molecular
> structures. It is through the monument or, one might rather say, among
> such imaginary scaffoldings as might be conceived to harmonise its conditions one with another – its purpose with stability, its proportions with
> its site, its form with its matter, and harmonising each of these conditions with
> itself, its millions of aspects among themselves, its types of balance among
> themselves, its three dimensions with one another, that we are best
> able to reconstitute the clear intelligence of a Leonardo. Such a mind can play
> at imagining the future sensations of the man who will make a circuit of
> the edifice, draw near, appear at a window, and by picturing what the man
> will see; or by following the weight of the roof as it is carried down
> walls and buttresses to the foundations; or by feeling the balanced stress of
> the beams and the vibration of the wind that will torment them; or by foreseeing the forms of light playing freely over the tiles and cornices,
> then diffused, encaged in rooms where the sun touches the floors. It will test
> and judge the pressure of the lintel on its supports, the expediency of
> the arch, the difficulties of the vaulting, the cascades of the steps gushing
> from their landings, and all the power of invention that terminates in a durable
> mass, embellished, defended, and made liquid with windows, made for

our lives, to contain our words, and out of it our smoke will rise.

    Architecture is commonly misunderstood. Our notion of it varies from stage setting to that of an investment in housing. I suggest we refer to the idea of the City in order to appreciate its universality, and that we should come to know its complex charm by recalling the multiplicity of its aspects. For a building to be motionless is the exception; our pleasure comes from movingabout it so as to make the building move in turn, while we enjoy all the combinations of its parts, as they vary: the column turns, depths recede, galleries glide; a thousand visions escape, a thousand harmonies.[4]

Once written, texts are like monuments; they need to stand still to allow our minds to move around them, and appreciate "the balanced stress of the beams and the vibration of the wind, which will torment them."[5]

    "A rose is a rose is a rose," and *The Architecture of the City* is the architecture of the city: It has built our image of a prototypical urban environment, it has helped us to give a bold form to a series of scattered realizations of the true nature of the built environment; bold and at the same time ever-changing, the beloved backdrop of our busy lives.

1   See, for example, the circular town planning schemes in Victor Gruen: *The heart of our cities: The urban crisis: diagnosis and cure,* New York, Simon and Schuster, 1964, the mathematical formulas and the discussion on modelling and urban planning in Leslie Martin and Lionel March editors, *Urban Space and Structures,* Cambridge University Press, London/New York, 1972, ISBN 0521084148, or the conceptual diagrams contained in Serge Chermayeff, Alexander Tzonis: *Shape of Community*
(Italian translation: *La forma dell'ambiente collettivo,* Il Saggiatore, Firenze 1972).

2   Walter Gropius, *"Flach-, Mittel- oder Hochbau?",* speech at the CIAM, in Rationelle Bebauungsweisen, 1931, pp. 26–47, English translation as Id., "Houses, Walk-ups or High-rise Apartment Blocks?", in *The Scope of Total Architecture,* MacMillan Publishing Company, New York, 1980.

3   "Beyond a certain critical mass each structure becomes a monument, or at least raises that expectation through its size alone, even if the sum or the nature of the individual activities it accommodates does not deserve a monumental expression. This category of monument presents a radical, morally traumatic break with the conventions of symbolism: its physical manifestation does not represent an abstract ideal, an institution of exceptional importance, a three-dimensional, readable articulation of a social hierarchy, a memorial; it merely is itself and through sheer volume cannot avoid being a symbol – an empty one, available for meaning as a billboard is for advertisement." Rem Koolhaas, *Delirious New York. A Retroactive Manifesto for Manhattan,* 1978, new edition: The Monacelli Press, New York 1994 ISBN 1885254·00 8, p. 100.

4   Paul Valéry, "Introduction à la méthode de Léonard de Vinci," in *La Nouvelle Revue,* 1895, pp. 742–770, English translation from Paul Valéry, *An Anthology, Selected, with an Introduction,* by James R.Lawler, edited by Jackson Mathews, Routledge & Kegan Paul, London and Henley, 1977 ISBN 071008806X, pp. 79–81.

5   Ibid.

98 ❙ The Ancient City

Giovanna Silva

Aleppo, 2007

Dead Palms

> A distinctive characteristic of all cities, and thus also of the urban aesthetic,
> is the tension that has been, and still is, created between areas
> and primary elements and between one sector of the city and another.
> This tension arises from the differences between urban artifacts
> existing in the same place and must be measured not only in terms of space
> but also of time. – Aldo Rossi, "Processes of Transformation"
> in *The Architecture of the City* (1966)

If it is true that the palm trees of Porto constitute a distinctive characteristic of the city and therefore of its urban aesthetic, then, following Rossi's hypothesis, one is in a good position to look into the history of tensions and processes of transformation that they convey.

The relation between palm trees and Portuguese culture can be traced as far back as 1808, when John VI, then Prince of the United Kingdom of Portugal, Brazil and the Algarves, relocated the court to Brazil, fleeing from Napoleonic Wars. That same year, John VI established the "Royal Nursery" garden – later to become the Botanic Garden of Rio de Janeiro – where in 1809, he himself planted the first seeds of imperial palm in Brazilian soil, smuggled from Mauritius by Portuguese merchant Luís Vieira e Silva while he was in transit from the Portuguese state of India, at that point part of the Portuguese Empire. The dissemination of the imperial palm in Brazil expressed the tensions of class structure in the then-overseas colony, just as it later would upon its arrival in mainland Portugal. Owned by the royal family and a symbol of Portuguese aristocracy, the first seeds of this "Palma Mater" were occasionally offered to selected noblemen for their services to the crown, but mostly burnt to preserve the exclusiveness and the status symbol associated with this species.

Naturally, such a restriction only made the imperial palm more desirable to the eyes of the emerging Brazilian bourgeoisie, a situation which soon gave rise to a black market for the seeds, fed by the gardeners of the Royal Nursery. By the mid-nineteenth century, the imperial palm was no longer an exclusive symbol of the aristocracy, but also a symbol of economic power, like a trademark for the coffee barons, properties of the Paraíba Valley. Portuguese cities and quite notably, Porto, were impacted by the strong wave of Brazilian immigration following the return of John VI and his court to Portugal in 1821 and Brazil's subsequent independence process.

Wealthy Brazilian return migrants settled in the oriental part of the city, away from the center, and undertook the urban expansion towards the east. Their unusually large mansions broke with the standard metric of the Porto plot and defined a new standard of luxury and status in the city. The imperial palms were one of the recognizable symbols of these properties, and just like decades before in Brazil, they expressed a new urban and social tension – one related to the upsurge of a new bourgeoisie with a craving for visibility, which would reconfigure urban form and local class structure. Of course in time, as palm trees spread across the urban territory and social structure of Porto, the original tension that they carried gave place to that of a collective symbol. Palm trees in Porto traveled across monarchic, republican, autocratic and democratic times. They spread into public space and institutional grounds, were objects of propaganda in the First Colonial Exhibition, and as they were liberalized, they were to be found in households of every socioeconomic class, in every neighborhood of the city. Pervasive as they became, standing out and above the cityscape, exotic among the local temperate flora, Porto palm trees shaped the collective memory of the city in the past two hundred years, and in so doing they have acquired historical importance and the unofficial status of monuments.

The arrival of the red palm weevil in Porto around 2010 has marked the beginning of a notorious process of urban transformation. The pest has attacked a great number of the city palms, and thus disfigured a distinctive attribute of the urban landscape. But as the corruption of these symbols anticipates its disappearance, the very process of putrefaction itself is elevating the monumental character of these elements.

Ursa:
Alexandre Delmar
Margarida Quintã
Luís Ribeiro da Silva

The lifeless bodies of dried fibers stand out in their spatial settings like they never did in their lush past, producing a powerful tension of decay that is breaking down the physical evidence of a culture and thus questioning the identity of the city.

Notes on Aldo Rossi's Geography and History; the Human Creation

The history of the city is always inseparable from its geography.
– Aldo Rossi, *The Architecture of the City,* p. 97

Rossi's interest in geography was not limited to the analytical framework it provides to describe the city. It expresses a deeper concern about the interrelations between architecture, territory and planning, which is very strongly developed in his writings of the early 1960s.[1] These texts already show a reaction to the modernist "ideology of planning," to use Tafuri's terminology, and an interest in articulating an architectural response to it. This response was aimed at fostering the collective and political dimension of space, in the belief that territory and planning were still the conditions that made any architectural project truly operative.

Rossi's first account of the autonomous dimension that urbanism and architecture can have is aimed at finding a specific role for these disciplines within the mostly economically driven processes of territorial planning. In the collective volume *Problemi sullo Sviluppo delle Aree Arretrate,* published in 1960, Rossi significantly starts his contribution with a critique of the totalizing meta-geographical approach represented by Le Corbusier for its lack of relation to particular realities.[2] He advocates, instead, for "elastic planning," which he defines as "a planning of wide spectrum (referring to an area that constitutes a culturally and geographically unitary nucleus) which understands the project, abandoned of all simplicity, as the articulation of a process open to the diverse requirements, more sensible towards the local historical values, analytic and decentralized."[3] Rossi argues that the autonomy of the architectural and urban discourse introduces, within the strict economic rationality of the plan, the possibility of articulating a political space. Following Carlo Cattaneo's work, this political space is referred to as a precise territorial realm: "The city forms with its regions an elementary body, this adhesion between the county and the city, constitutes a political persona, permanent and inseparable."[4]

In *Problemi sullo Sviluppo delle Aree Arretrate,* Rossi considers that this territorial, political space could be articulated through a new form of settlement: an architectural complex which, joining residence with industry, production with habitation, would show the occupation of the region by a new political collectivity. In his subsequent writings, Rossi abandons this functional idea to consider, instead, that commercial and industrial buildings, infrastructures and the like, constitute the elements that actually organize the territorial scale, while housing becomes an almost negligible element. What remains through this change of uses is the understanding that only architectural fragments can articulate the territory.

In this sense, the crucial differentiation between primary element and area – where the latter is predominantly residential – that Rossi establishes in *The Architecture of the City* can be seen as originating not in the city, but in the territory. Even if the notion of the primary element, so central in the book, is the element that "characterizes a city" and the carrier of its architectural value, it certainly transcends the scale of the architectural object. In Rossi's words, a primary element "can be seen as an actual urban artefact, identifiable with an event or an architecture that is capable of 'summarising' the city."[5] In a time where the definition of the urban has come into crisis, when extended urbanization processes have taken a planetary dimension, more than looking at the city as a traditionally bounded, compact and distinct formal structure, it may be pertinent to look back at the intertwined relations between architecture and geography, or in other words, at the construction of the territory as a "human creation," with all its cultural, political and geographical dimensions. The city Rossi was trying to encapsulate in his theory was composed of a varied, complex and rich architectural imagery, reaching beyond the historic and modern repertoire of formal articulations. By broadening its classical definition, we may conclude that the form of the city is to be associated with its geography, its routes, highways and other

Adrià Carbonell
Roi Salgueiro Barrio

Nineteenth century engraving of the Ponte del Diavolo on the St. Gotthard Pass Switzerland, by R. Dikenmann. Nature and man's construction.

infrastructures, the irrigation of fields and industrial settlements; thus, the form of the city would actually be the form of its territory. In this sense, Rossi participates in a generational concern; yet, unlike some of his contemporaries – like Saverio Muratori or Vittorio Gregotti, who investigated how geography could contaminate architectural and urban form – the a priori formal autonomy of architecture that Rossi claims has the capacity to determine how the territory is going to be perceived and how it is going to be culturally and politically articulated. This may be one of the lessons we owe to Rossi's *The Architecture of the City,* a book about the city that opens with the image of a bridge in the territory.

1   With regards to Rossi's account of the relationship between architecture, territory and planning, it's interesting to note the evolution of his thesis from the position he held in the contribution written together with Silvano Tintori in 1960 for the collective volume *Problemi sullo sviluppo delle aree arretrate (Problems about the Development of Depressed Areas)*, to the 1962 paper "New Problems", to *The Architecture of the City,* published in 1966.
2   The volume was intended to continue the intellectual work initiated in the 1954 International Symposium of Underdeveloped Areas, held in Milan, in which Le Corbusier participated. For Le Corbusier, a metageographical analysis was the basis of a theoretical model: one that could reconfigure France after World War II, but also the totality of Europe, to use his expression: "from the Alps to the Urals."
3   Aldo Rossi and Silvano Tintori, "Aspettiurbanistici del problemadelle zone arretrate in Italia e in Europa" in *Problemi sullo sviluppo delle aree arretrate,* ed. Ajmone Marsan, V., Giovanni Demaria, and Centro Nazionale Di Prevenzionee di Difesa Sociale (Bologna: 1960), 248–9. Our translation.
4   Aldo Rossi and Silvano Tintori, op. cit., 251–252. Our translation.
5   Aldo Rossi, *The Architecture of the City* (Cambridge, MA: The MIT Press, 1984) p. 99.

104 Ⅲ **The *Locus***

229 Stefano Graziani

Menhir, Carnac, 2015, Brittany, France (da Carnac or Alignements)

Post-Critical Urbanism

When the villager had to get water from the village square fountain or food from the marketplace, social and political life was born in the city. Villagers didn't arbitrarily choose to gather for a chat in open spaces, outside the shelter of their homes. Similarly, the arcade was invented to protect inhabitants from snow or sun. The air pollution in century cities gave rise to boulevards for ventilation which, consequently, caused new social behaviors like strolling. These fundamental causes of urban design were ignored during the twentieth century thanks to the enormous use of energy by pumps, motors, refrigeration, heating systems and air conditioning, which cause today's greenhouse effect.

Overcoming the legacies of energy, food and climatic constraints, urban theory from the 1970s, like Aldo Rossi's Tendenza and American Pop Art, led to cities that have been designed in response to only social and cultural values, which are really the effects of urban form rather than its causes. Out of this came a tendency for urban designers and architects to use a morpho-typological analysis of the city, wherein they study and repeat more or less precisely the formal drawing and figurative language of the city in its current state, regardless of climate or physiological necessity.

Following this logic, the designers of urban form sought to understand the "spirit of place," its formal and material identity, and to establish a plastic and cultural language — making use of a grammar based on semantic reference, analogy, allusion and narration — which propagates, more or less, deviance, irony and nostalgia. This analytical method slowly emerged in the 1960s as an architectural extension of the critical philosophical theories proposed as a response to the disaster of World War II (1939–45), such as Adorno and Horkheimer's critical theory coming from the Frankfurt School or Foucault's postmodernism in France, deeply disillusioned by the progressive and scientific objectives of the modernity of the early twentieth century.

Modernity began, full of hope, as a mechanism through which mankind could progress and find happiness. It ended with the bloodshed of World War II and the atomic bomb. Since the late 1960s, critical theories have denounced philosophers' ideas of progress — technical, scientific or architectural — accusing them of being responsible for the world's disasters. The critical theories in architecture instead favored linguistic and semantic analysis that evolved from the post-modern economical affluence of the end of the twentieth century and the development of tourism, a perfect match.

We have seen in recent years the exhaustion of critical methods, which actually had the effect of stifling architectural invention with repetition and formalism. By banishing the scientific and medical tools, they had only to focus on the narrative and plastic discourse, choosing the subjective over the objective and obscuring the physiological and climatic causes of urbanization. These methodologies, however, lack the tools and theory to adequately address the very immediate issues of global warming and dwindling natural resources. How can we respond to global warming with irony? Why tell a story about the depletion of resources instead of fighting it? We think today that science is not the cause of the catastrophes of the twentieth century but it was its use in a univocal, political way, without accepting difference, alterity and multiplicity, that was the cause.

Our position is in no way a return to the genesis of our modernity, but rather a generation of a new phase of architectural history that is post-post-modern, or maybe "post-critical," as defined Hal Foster in his essay "Post-Critical"[1]. We want to reengage physiology and meteorology as new tools for urban and architectural design, in thinking critically by welcoming the multiplicity, diversity, and alterity of spaces and atmospheres, embracing the comfortable and uncomfortable, hot and cold, good and bad, wet and dry, clean and polluted, and the gradations between these extremes, to allow the user the freedom to use and interpret spaces in order to ensure his or her free will.

We want to abandon the modern, univocal vision of space. We do not want to design uniform atmospheres that would only provide so-called perfect climates,

Philippe Rahm

because we also want free choice for everybody between colder or warmer spaces, sunny or cloudy, clean or polluted. In this sense, we are the heirs of critical thinking, and not the neo-modern. Our goal is to re-engage science, medicine and technology with critical thinking, and to expand the toolset of critical thinking to include medical tools and physiological analyses. Our design brings a variety of atmospheres and a diversity of situations into the outdoor and indoor spaces, abandoning the so-called perfect and the univocal, controlled modern architecture, keeping the field of architectural design as open as possible, diversified, multiple, by accepting and designing either so-called good or less good places. Thus, the future of architecture and urbanism is post-critical.

We need to reengage the basic physiological and climatic necessities of the contemporary world in order to invent a new urban language, new forms and urban spaces to address these needs and raise new political, social and cultural behaviors.

(III) Urban Ecology and Psychology

Arriving at San Cataldo, from America, from an American childhood and architectural education, tests the boundaries of associative thinking. The echoes are embarrassingly close to home. Driving from northwest of Modena, the cemetery appears over the gentle rise of a highway ramp. The pastel mass of its pitched metal roof aligns with overhead power lines. There is a bus stop and a parking lot. It is surprising how big the buildings are, how wide and how tall. How the windows, so stark black in Rossi's famous watercolors, are framed in the pale blue-green of the roof, and divided into four parts by conspicuous mullions.

A few people get off the bus holding flowers. The effect of the place before you falls short of the uncanny purity of Rossi's painted forms. The disconnect between expectation and experience makes space for a strange flash of association – you could mistake it for America, for a vast complex of stucco buildings surrounded by highways, a pilgrimage site of sorts out in the suburbs. It almost looks like a shopping mall. The association feels crass – a disservice to Rossi's impeccable sense of monument, context, history, and program, and to the solemnity of the place – and it fades as you walk around. But the core of it sticks with you: a crossing of wires brought on by an unexpected, buried body of personal experience. A mundane, essentially American memory of the city layering itself, unbidden, onto an Italian icon.

Memory, and the ways that memory locates itself within or grafts itself onto physical artifacts, are essential concepts in *The Architecture of the City.* "'The soul of the city' becomes the city's history," Rossi writes, "…One can say that the city itself is the collective memory of its people."[1] Collective memory is the stuff from which the city is built, the force that defines the artifacts that structure the urban. But Rossi is less interested in the psychology and memory of the individual citizen, or the non-citizen visitor. Underneath the book's 20th sub-heading, "Urban Ecology and Psychology," he dissociates architectural thinking from psychological feeling: "When Bernini speaks disdainfully of Paris because he finds its Gothic landscape barbarous, we are hardly interested in Bernini's psychology; instead we are interested in the judgment of an architect who on the basis of the total and specific culture of one city judges the structure of another city."[2]

But when you get there, to San Cataldo, sitting on a bench between the blank yellow stucco walls and the famous, hollow-eyed cube, it is easier to put yourself into Bernini's shoes. It is not possible to shake the suburban scale of the place, or the rush of the highway so nearby. You are in Modena, on the edge of an ancient city, but you are also home, in upstate New York, or driving across Indiana. You are standing at the edge of a housing subdivision, looking over a corrugated metal gate into the adjoining hayfield. There is the rumbling discomfort of wide open spaces.

The power of collective memories and spaces is that they gather individual stories, that they provide an image and a canvas that is constantly, productively refracted through the assembled histories of those that pass through. They provoke comparison, discussion and framing that allow disparate forces to come together without the pressure of consensus. Rather than drawing on "the total and specific culture of one city," at San Cataldo, you are invited to examine your own fragmentary, reconstituted recollections. By its peculiar, unwelcome, awkward scale and raw unfinishedness, you are reminded that artifacts, collectives, need not be whole or seamless, and that "the judgment of an architect" is always rooted in personal and interpersonal narrative.

San Cataldo is a product of Modena, of the study of its history, its people, of the history of the European city, of the Italian landscape. Every day it is a venue for people to remember the dead, to stand in silence at their engraved names, and to return home on the bus. But part of the uncanny power of the place comes from the ease with which it sheds that specificity – how it welcomes and dissolves into images brought from other countries, traditions, and times. At points in *The Architecture of the City,* Rossi's attempt at scientific rigor feels forced. His watercolors are the inverse, raw emotion distorting and smearing his clean forms, shadows deepening to harsh black. Eisenman argues that the drawings are the true locus of Rossi's architecture, preserving space for fantasy amidst cities over-determined by history and layered form. But for an American visitor at San Cataldo, the building itself – half-built, too big, stranded on the edge of the city – allows for an ambiguity and space for thought that is not achieved by either the book or the drawings.

1   Aldo Rossi, *The Architecture of the City,* trans. Diane Ghirardo and Joan Ockman (Cambridge: MIT Press, 1982), 130.
2   Rossi, *City,* 114.

Rossi the Ambiguous

Thirty underground parking spaces. How to best arrange thirty underground parking spaces? What about the width of the corridor so that two people can pass, and the distance to the lift shaft? How many square meters are the offices, what is the size of the canteen, how big is the lobby, what proportion is the facade to the floor area? How big is the plaza, what is the width of the pavement beyond the plaza, what is the footprint of the building in the master plan, how many trees are in the streets (are there trees?), what is the distance to the bus stop, the city center, the airport, the suburb?

So pick up your Neufert, your guidebook to the actual. The logic that informs it is the foundation to our regulations, our planning, our designs. The world it describes presents neutrality as a style, an ideal device for fixing in place the invisible bureaucratic forces that form the city. Its generalized solutions set out each and every point of life as a discrete problem, from the completely public to the deeply private. It has come to describe how to live rather than how we might be minimally comfortable. It describes that things need not be any more than this, nor any less than that. Efficiency as the primary generator of space. This is the condition within which we live.

And if efficiency was not the starting point? There have been and could be other priorities, impulses and ideas.

The point at which bureaucratic technocracy becomes not just a useful assistant in making our cities, but the very spirit, style and character of our environment is the point when we must wonder if this is what we want. By focusing on discrete guidelines and solutions, Neufert and its close family members, regulation and standardization, have led to a technique of hyper-specificity that results in vague places. Rossi, in his *Architecture of the City,* attempts the opposite: ambiguous discourse asking for specific qualities to be designed into places. It resists being what it is, a book of guidelines for designers, resisting for the sake of not becoming a deadening, closed system.

I have no argument with standard building processes and materials. I make no argument that Rossi rally against them. I love these things; my practice revolves around them, and I would argue that Rossi's did too. In *The Architecture of the City,* Rossi is asking us to see what other ingredients make a city that go beyond data.

The Architecture of the City is written from a designer's point of view. Its chapters describe the designer's concerns; it is for the architect tackling something that will be made physical in the world. Who are these decisions for? Whose duty is it to care? How can a design be precise and concrete, yet adaptable in use and non-oppressive? The book can be seen as the result of a productive anxiety over the responsibility of these decisions. Rossi does not hide from the monumental scale of collective experience that the city requires.

The desire to write and theorize about what propels *The Architecture of the City* comes as one epoch is ending and another starting. It was the forbearer of other seminal books that hoped to respond to the supposed death of modernism: first *Learning from Las Vegas,* then *Delirious New York.* Each of these books set out to learn from existing cities and build a foundation from which to design in relation to the qualities of "city", as they saw it, rather than to design discrete objects (potentially culturally and socially irrelevant). The later books are written with America as the subject, and aim to resolve a then-tense desire for relevance by theorizing an American vernacular city form as a new paradigm (these theories later become their design work). The authors aimed to supersede the seminal books that preceded their own as manifestos. Rossi's book is written with Europe as its subject, and aims to resolve the perceived diminishing force of modernism by pointing to the vernacular qualities of European historical cities as a petri dish of examples. Rossi does not aim to supersede, but rather wants to find a way to work with both architecture as a continuous and independent body of knowledge developed over thousands of years and the political left's project to spread equality (which of course must view historical social forms as bondage).

Rossi's book is looking to resolve this seeming contradiction as a basis for his design work. He finds a way to satisfy himself by settling on a kind of continuation of the work of the first generation of "true" modern architects. This was a generation, perhaps the final one, that had a truly classical education. The relevance of this is that their work was a hybrid between the historical forms they had learnt and the raw abstraction they were looking for. In this sense, Rossi was not post-modern like his contemporaries who worked with the fine plastic details and games of falsity from high classical architectural systems. His work is primarily based on unadorned primary forms and elements, with a more archaic, more proletarian, more infrastructural quality. It recalls Piranesi's *Antichità Romane* more than Palladianism. The results of his attempt at a resolution between architectural history and leftist politics has been adopted both consciously and unconsciously by parts of each subsequent generation: in some cases wanting to replicate the qualities of a traditional city as opposed to continuing the spatial experiments of postwar modernism, and in some cases wishing to recall the rawness of archaic temples and ancient infrastructural wonders. Purposefully dense, architecturally direct, intellectually ambitious, the ideas Rossi set forward in The *Architecture of the City* hold great power today. And yet in his book he wriggles as much as possible out of allowing one to follow his texts as a set of commandments. This is perhaps the most powerful quality of the work.

112 Ⅲ The Roman Forum

Annette Amberg

Annette Amberg, roma, 2013, film still. Courtesy of the artist.

The City of Architecture

Reading Aldo Rossi's *The Architecture of the City,* one feels a constant sense of being only one step away from suggestive, however elusive, conclusions. With its inserts and shifts, rethinkings and omissions (still partly perceptible), the text clearly shows Rossi's effort to enunciate an intuitive and poetic thought in rigorous and deductive terms, aiming at the construction of an "urban science." This is why *The Architecture of the City* is a palimpsest: each explicit word has a corresponding hidden one. The subchapter "Monuments: Summary of the Critique of the Concept of Context" is no exception. In order to follow the discourse, it is necessary to trace some virtual parentheses or notes, unravel formulations that are so dense as to sound unfathomable, presuppose passages that have been lost along the way, perceive the imminent presence of undeclared sources, and shuffle around incoherent sequences into the right order.

In the last lines of the previous subchapter, "The Roman Forum," Rossi repeated his intention to understand the city as "pre-eminently a collective fact." He now intends to carry out his "Critique of the Concept of Context" precisely in order to answer a question (although unformulated) that could be derived from the previous affirmation: if the city "is of an essentially collective nature," which is the specific role that architecture plays in it?

Everything becomes clearer once we accept that this is the question that Rossi seeks to answer. Rossi's argument stems from the contrast between "context" and "monument." The point is that this is a contrast that should logically drive him to recalibrate the function of architecture: if context and monument are opposites, and context must prevail in the city (the nature of which is "collective"), architecture is useless. Not willing to reach this conclusion, Rossi is required to avoid the contrast altogether. This is why the entire paragraph reads as a defense of the "peculiar" and "singular" role that something like architecture holds in the construction of something "collective" like a city. Indeed, *The Architecture of the City.*

Anyone expecting a following argument on this point will be, however, let down. Yet, after many circumvolutions, Rossi's answer does finally arrive. The topic of the book, as Rossi himself states, is "architecture as a component of the urban artifact;" and "it would be foolish," he continues, "to think that the problem of architecture can be [...] revealed through a context or a purported extension of a context's parameters." It would be foolish, since "context is specific precisely in that it is constructed through architecture."

Here is where Rossi meant to arrive. He had already declared his agreement with authors who considered the city "pre-eminently a collective fact", but he now wants to emphasize the fact that his conclusions diverge from those derived by others from similar premises. Architecture – freely paraphrasing Rossi – cannot be deducted from context (which, in Rossi's terms, has a negative connotation: it is a "pathological permanence"). The city, he writes, is not built by means of establishing a general rule (deducted from context) and applying it to a particular case (like architecture), but on the contrary, by assuming that the latter should be the fundamental "component" of the city. Rossi had already expressed his opinion on this: "The assumption that urban artifacts are the founding principle of the cities denies and refuses the notion of urban design." To the coexistent tendency of conceiving the city as following "volumetric-quantitative" standards, he coherently responds with the necessity to start from the building, "in the most concrete way possible."

Following the logic of this paragraph, some affirmations make their way through other pages of the book and assume singular relevance, in particular: "Architecture becomes, by extension, the city." In these words resonates an allusion – that seems to never have been noted – to a famous sentence that is present in the treatises of Leon Battista Alberti and Andrea Palladio, picked up (among others) by Durand in a fragment that is quoted in the book but most likely mediated by one of Rossi's contemporaries. Aldo van Eyck had been repeating, for years, that "house is city and city is house." He had first stated it in Otterlo and repeated it in *Domus.* But what was a

Daniele Pisani

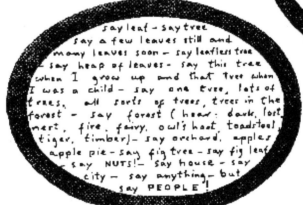

Aldo van Eyck, Tree is Leaf and Leaf is Tree, 1962

chiasm for van Eyck becomes, however, a unilateral assertion for Rossi: city is not house, but *house is city.* The city shall be the objective of architecture "The whole is more important than the single parts", but it's the architecture that makes the city, not the opposite.

    Rossi is trying to affirm that the architectural project's rational capacity to "foresee" is not unlimited. In his view, the world is complex; architecture is part of a play in which many actors are involved and, once built, does not belong to itself any longer. The fact is that architecture implies an instance of order that inevitably collides with those of others and with the *locus.* It is indeed from this conflict that *la chose humaine par excellence* originates: the city. Indeed, is it not Rossi himself who claims that his book "is not concerned with architecture in itself but with architecture as a component of the urban artifact?" The City of Architecture.

The City as History, History as Life

Since the mid-eighties, Rossi's professional activity becomes hectic. The blue notebooks record faithfully the intellectual and physical commitment required by the amount of work Rossi undergoes. In particular, those written between 1989 and 1991 contain several intimate notes (...). Their tone is not surprising, while the literary style and writing reveal haste, impatience, moments of instability and neglect. (...). These pages represents the end of an intellectual and existential cycle dating back to the beginning of Rossi's career. In 1973 Rossi writes: "The last time we had dinner together in Milan one sentence struck me: the advantage to start drinking in the morning is to be subtly drunk without ever being really drunk. When I was young I thought it was important to be really out of control, a total collapse. Now I listen and stay: through a growing deafness abstraction is tinged by a sense of presence. It may be the disappointment of a brilliant man, but perhaps only the condition an old man."[1]

Rossi won the Pritzker prize in 1990. The ceremony was held in Venice on June 16th, at Palazzo Grassi. In July, Rossi moved his Milanese office from Via Maddalena to Via Santa Maria alla Porta. The building, at No. 9, directly faces the baroque facade of the church of Santa Maria alla Porta designed by Francesco Maria Richini. The office's international notoriety grew together with the number of commissions. The office needed a bigger and more central space. There were many things happening in Rossi's life in those years. "The time that slips through your fingers became more and more rapidly the focus of the blue notebooks. (...) A melancholy also imprinted Rossi's physical traits, similar to those Theodor W. Adorno observed in Chaplin, 'He entered the scene as if continuing a long walk.'"[2] A drastic mutation characterizes the texts Rossi wrote during that period: there is a shift that gradually transforms Rossi's prose through a renewed poetic trigger together with an increasing interest in death, memory, fragments, analogy as key elements of his narrative. A reverse relationship flipped Rossi's career: on the one hand, the interest in writing as a form of memory – be it books, essays or project reports – kept growing, while on the other hand there was a declining interest in architecture as an analytical and rational operation, as if Rossi increasingly permeated the *logic construction of architecture* through autobiographical or extrinsic traits. The city was no longer a juxtaposition of multiple layers sedimented through collective efforts but it became a set of highly personal memories, far from the structure – though chaotic – provided by the theory of urban facts contained in *The Architecture of the City.* In the introduction to the last volume that Alberto Ferlenga dedicated to his work, Rossi wrote: "I omitted the great treatises for more than one reason: mainly for a certain idealism that separates them from restlessness; for a sort of self-confidence the treatises inexorably force architecture into a demiurgical process that intersects with politics: from the height of Alberti to the aggressive urbanism of Le Corbusier; they above all claim to offer an order to life."[3] Rossi reads the city through a different take in respect to his juvenile one: through A *Scientific Autobiography*[4] Rossi registers things without any tension, taking notes before the farewell. A much more intimate and disenchanted position than the one proposed in the early works, ideology – or maybe idealism – leaves space for a repository of memories: private diaries programmatically written – and scripted – for the use and consumption of the reader.

> Everything drifted into autobiography. The collective spectres turned into private spectres. The figures of memory no longer made any effort to be shared, subjected to the wear and tear of language, to betrayals of meaning.[5]

Nicolò Ornaghi

A *Scientific Autobiography* does not present specific tools for understanding the contemporary city; nonetheless, it allows us to grasp some elements of the *private archive* from which Rossi constituted his late architectures. Those architectures demonstrate the interference of a private sphere in a collective dimension and the substitution of an objective and shared complexity with an autobiographical and private set of images. Rossi certainly, after his first successful book, no longer provided *instructions* – neither for the city nor for architecture. Instead, he started to transfer upon himself the complexity of the city by moving between the rational and the subjective, transforming urban complexity into autobiographical narrative. The book, as well as the diaries, are instruments of memory through which it is possible to understand the relationship between the architect and his standpoints recurring throughout his career and, above all, his life. They testify a certain irrelevance as architecture if compared to life, as well as Rossi's rightful obsession with life, which, in the end, "means much more than architecture."[6] The architectures produced are thus apparently empty, surely indifferent to program and function. Architectures that are reticent, desolate and obscure. "… Your projects without objectivity, alluding to meanings which are suddenly deprived, which refuse the world, they are precisely acts of 'private poetry,' the less mystifying the more they stay locked in their hermetic silence."[7] These architectures define the space of the inner world of the architect but they no longer have the ambition to change the space they settle in. They represent the life of the author; that is their only history.

1   Aldo Rossi to Carlo Aymonino, October 5th, 1973, Archivio Carlo Aymonino. In F. Dal Co, *Il Teatro della Vita,* pg. XVII, XVIII. In Aldo Rossi, F. Dal Co (a cura di) *I quaderni azzurri,* Mondadori Electa, Milano, 1999. Translation by the author.
2   F. Dal Co, *Il Teatro della Vita,* pg. XIX. Aldo Rossi, F. Dal Co (a cura di), I quaderni azzurri, Mondadori Electa, Milano, 1999. Translation by the author.
3   A. Rossi, *Un'oscura innocenza*. In A.Ferlenga, *Aldo Rossi,* architetture 1993–1996, Opera completa vol.II, Mondadori Electa, Milano, 1996, p. 9. Translation by the author
4   A.Rossi, *A Scientific Autobiography,* MIT Press, Cambridge, Mass., 1981.
5   Baukuh, *Two Essays on Architecture,* Kommode Verlag, Zürich, 2014, p. 64. (Due saggi sull'architettura, Sagep editori, Genova, 2012)
6   "He was rightfully obsessed with life, which means much more than architecture. Sometimes life dresses up as architecture, but to understand architecture it is better to understand life first. Otherwise you are in a game of styles. You ride – or risk riding – some watchwords without truly understanding them, watchwords that only trends can impose. After all, architecture lives on trends, always has. Like any human manifestation, like how we dress, architecture is a permanent dress that we ourselves wear. It is fatally subject to fashion, but we need to be aware that these trends are temporary, and that the only real need is to be covered." Arduino Cantafora in Nicolò Ornaghi, Francesco Zorzi, "A conversation with Arduino Cantafora." Log 35, Fall 2015, p. 94
7   Manfredo Tafuri to Aldo Rossi, 12 ottobre 1971, *Rossi Papers*. Translation by the author.

118 Ⅲ The Collective Memory

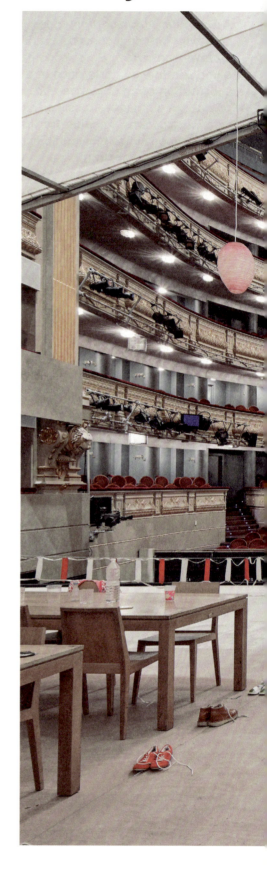

Walter Mair

Wozzeck, Opera by Alban Berg, Teatro Real, Madrid 2013. Sylvain Cambreling, Conductor; Christoph Marthaler, Stage Director; Anna Viebrock, Set and Costume Design; Olaf Winter, Lighting

Wozzeck, Opera by Alban Berg, Teatro Real, Madrid 2013. Sylvain Cambreling, Conductor; Christoph Marthaler, Stage Director; Anna Viebrock, Set and Costume Design; Olaf Winter, Lighting

Two Reverse Urban Artifacts in Athens

The modern Greek state was founded in 1828, after about four centuries of Ottoman rule over its territory. In 1834, Athens was chosen as its capital, triggering a series of archaeological and architectural projects that aimed to reaffirm and restore its ancient past. This new city was certainly different from the ancient Athens that Rossi described in *The Architecture of the City,* but it fed from the same myth: it reproduced the image of classical monuments in modern Neoclassical compositions of stucco. Meanwhile, the actual matter of its heritage, the ancient marbles, were progressively protected, sanitized and kept safely within guarded archaeological sites and museums.

Such uses of the classical were radically different from what happened in the city before the occurrence of scientific archaeology and the concept of a "national heritage." In previous centuries, the classical was utilized in more direct ways, as the people of Athens appropriated marble pieces of ancient monuments and used them, structurally or decoratively, in their own vernacular constructions. Whereas nineteenth-century neoclassicism used the classical as a consistent theoretical apparatus, this pre-modern makeshift "classicism" used the classical as fragment, surrounding it with mythical interpretations and adapting it to new architectural and significational purposes.

Within this context, two neighboring buildings can serve as reverse "urban artifacts," reaffirming and hopefully extending Rossi's analysis.

The Metropolitan Cathedral of Athens (fig. 1) was an ambitious project initiated by the Bavarian King Otto, Greece's first Bavarian monarch, as an attempt to appease the Christian Orthodox populace of the city. Otto's planners at first wanted to situate the building along one of the city's main monumental axes; Panepistimiou Avenue, which already included other public institutions, such as the city's university, library and academy. But eventually, they opted instead for a site closer to the buzzing old core of the city. Construction began in the 1840s, but it took about three architects and 20 years for its completion. More importantly, its construction required the re-use of materials from about 72 demolished buildings. Nevertheless, nothing in the building's neoclassical symmetry, uniform decoration and stucco exterior gave away traces of its heterogeneous construction.

At the time, European neoclassicism was imported as the ultimate "local" style for Greece, as it "returned" to its place of origin. In the case of the cathedral, this strategy of nation-building was further refined by incorporating elements of the country's Byzantine heritage: Orthodox Christianity, for which Greeks had previously fought against the Ottomans, was now housed in a building whose architecture blended the Neoclassical style with several Byzantine details, altogether in the form of an occidental cathedral. Its location and monumentality are indicative of an intention to create an urban artifact: the cathedral was designed as an indicator of form, style and scale for the re-shaping of Athens in the nineteenth century.

Right next to this cathedral stands a tiny church (fig. 2) which displays a strikingly different use of the material remains of the same myth of the classical: the Church of Gorgoepikoos (also known as *St. Eleftherios* and *Old Metropolitan Church*) was built in the eleventh century CE, but refurbished several times afterwards). The church adheres to the cross-in-square typology, but its exterior surface is a rather peculiar composition: its outer walls are clad in marble pieces, many of which are "spolia" (re-used architectural parts) from Hellenistic and classical monuments.

At the time of its construction, the building was densely surrounded by other buildings, within the city's labyrinthic medieval core. But these were destroyed to make space for the adjacent cathedral and piazza, leaving the small church to stand out as a rather alien object. Nevertheless, its scale and form are still indicative of the architectural logic of the city before the nineteenth century. Unlike its monumental neighbor, this pre-modern construction is not the materialization of an image drawn

Nikos Magouliotis

(fig. 1) The Athens Cathedral. Photograph by Pascal Sebah in 1874.
(fig. 2) The church of St. Eleftherios. Photograph by Ernst Reisinger in 1923.

on paper – i.e, a "design." It is, instead, a result of circumstances and specificities: decorative pieces, adorned with pagan imagery, were extracted from ancient monuments and incorporated into its construction, often altered to create a highly complicated urban artifact:

Above the main entrance (fig. 3) stands a relief which we now know to be a calendar, depicting the annual customs of Athenians in antiquity. But the church was built long before the era of scientific archaeology and preservation. Thus, its builders did not treat this relic with preservationist caution, but with an additive vandalism which attempted to transform its pictorial surface and its meaning: by carving crosses at specific intervals along its length, they displaced its semiotic towards Christianity and perhaps claimed that what was depicted was a sequence of Orthodox, and not Pagan customs.

Similarly, a plate encased in the north wall (fig. 4) depicting a naked, bearded man – somewhat reminiscent of a satyr – was "Christanized" through creative alteration: the two human figures that stood on each side of the naked man – possibly dancing nymphs – were replaced by two big crosses. His penis was also scraped off, and there you have it: what could once have been a dionysian figure is now an ascetic hermit, perfectly tailored to the exterior of a Christian church.

Finally, above the southern entrance (fig. 5) sits a marble relief which, according to later interpretations, contains symbols of the obscure Eleusinian rituals: a decorated head of a bull (which was usually sacrificed in such ceremonies), a shield with torches and a vessel that possibly contained the hallucinatory seeds consumed by the participants. Paradoxically, in this case, no alteration was made to the relief's imagery when it was re-used; the pagan ritualistic symbols were simply placed on the exterior of a Christian church.

One the one hand, the Athenians of the time had probably little knowledge of the obscurity contained in their ancient heritage. On the other, their religious practices were also not fully cleansed of such pagan remains, so they did not see such imagery as incompatible with their faith. Many of the spolia that were re-used to decorate such churches appear to have been valued more for their general aesthetic and material appeal and less for their particular meaning. People would also often assign magical powers and mythical interpretations to such relics, thus further reinventing and appropriating their meaning.

As stated previously, the Metropolitan Cathedral is a rather typical example of a building that was intended to function as an urban artifact, quite close to the way Rossi meant it. But for the case of Gorgoepikoos, this function is extended to what we could call an "urban signifier:" By using material fragments of the myth of the city, this small artifact absorbs, transforms and emits meaning; It transforms the city's history and deflects its potential meanings.

If seen in this way, it is perhaps not surprising that Gorgoepikoos appeared in Robert Venturi, Denise Scott-Brown and Steven Izenours's legendary *Learning from Las Vegas.* In the chapter on "Historical and Other Precedents," the church is described briefly as an "absurd [...] piece of architecture" and eventually categorized as both a "decorated shed" and a "duck." In one of the following spreads of the book (fig. 6), a photograph of Gorgoepikoos is subversively placed next to the Amiens Cathedral and the Golden Nugget Casino in Las Vegas. In the image credits of the book, the photo is credited to Robert Venturi, proving that the authors had visited it in previous years. The church is, somewhat imprecisely, referred to as "Metropole Cathedral," but it is clear that Venturi et al scorned the adjacent cathedral and focused, instead, on Gorgoepikoos. This brief reference appears to be the book's only mention of a building in Greece. If compared to Le Corbusier's *Vers une Architecture,* whose only Greek reference is the Parthenon, we could be led to a much wider discussion on modern and post-modern "historical precedents."

At this point, before declaring Gorgoepikoos to be a manifesto of "pre-modern post-modernism," we ought to return to how it relates to its aforementioned neighbor: Gorgoepikoos appears to be the result of architectural and constructional pragmatism, while the Athens Cathedral is a highly idealistic project. The two neighboring buildings relate to the idea of the urban artifact, but in very different ways: if the latter is an intentionally and consistently designed urban artifact, the former is a more haphazard retaining of history through the recycling of the architectural and mythical matter of the city.

But the opposition of these two urban artifacts manifests in one more way, which could overturn the analysis we attempted previously, as the church of Gorgoepikoos possesses a strong idealism underneath its "pragmatist" surface: its neighboring cathedral was built at a time of major urban reformation and it had to be aligned to the adjacent street. Forming a consistent grid of streets was more important than ecclesiastical dogma and thus, its apse is not perfectly orientated to the east. Conversely, Gorgoepikoos' apse is more precisely east-oriented, referring more to religious tradition than to the city around it. Despite its humble scale and its seemingly haphazard appearance, Gorgoepikoos is not only an urban, but also a cosmological artifact.

IV. The City as Field of Application for Various Forces: Economics

Several theorists have asserted that state ownership of property – that is, the abolition of private property – constitutes the qualitative difference between the capitalist city and the socialist one. This position is undeniable, but does it relate to urban artefacts? I am inclined to believe that it does, since the use and availability of land are fundamental issues – however, it still seems only a condition – a necessary condition, to be sure, but not a determining one.

One of the things that is often forgotten about many of the Italian architectural theorists and practitioners of the 1960s and 1970s is just how many of them were card-carrying members of, or at the very least sympathizers with, either the Communist Party of Italy or its splinter groups even further to the left. Accordingly, when Rossi, Tafuri, Dal Co, Cacciari, Superstudio or Archizoom write about property relations and their effect on the city, they're writing in a scenario where they believe it is both possible and desirable that private property, especially land, be totally abolished. Much of the work that is occasionally interpreted as goofy futurism – such as Superstudio's Continuous Monument with its mirror-glass grid sweeping the globe – is anti-capitalist satire. And much of what can easily be seen as Adorno-like Grand Hotel Abyss pessimism – Tafuri's scathing analysis of modernism's approach to social reform – is intended as a cautionary distinction between what is capitalism, however tamed and tempered, and what is socialism.

However, one of the many things going on in *The Architecture of the City* is an analysis of just how deep the roots of the city, the "urban question" and even, to a degree, the "housing problem" go: deeper by far than those of capitalism, which is a social formation that did not truly emerge until the eighteenth century, even if its bourgeoisie can be traced back a few centuries earlier than that. While some on the left – William Morris, for instance – occasionally seemed to think that urbanism, beyond a miniature, medieval level, was inherently capitalist, the existence of several pre-capitalist megalopoli belies this belief. But then this elicits a question, one that Rossi only hints at.

In his actual architectural practice, Rossi often took an approach which seemed to deliberately evoke the authoritarian architecture of the interwar years, whether the stripped down, rationalized, chilled classicism of Rome's EUR or, conceivably, the more decorative but similarly imposing and classically rooted architecture of the Stalinist Soviet Union and its satellites. Elsewhere, Rossi described the bloated, mutant Hausmannism of Berlin's Stalinallee (now Karl-Marx-Allee) as "Europe's Last Great Street." Sure, but was it a socialist street, and did its lack of capitalist land ownership lead to any real qualitative difference? Did it function differently, was it structured differently, was it haptically or spatially different from anything built by the bourgeoisie, by property speculators, or even by social-democratically inclined local authorities? Or did it resemble the urbanism of the sort of power that actually predates capitalism, such as absolutism, feudalism or slavery? Naturally, Rossi refuses to be drawn into such matters, having only made a design preference for an approach to form with some unpleasant associations. The embrace of the historic city, meanwhile, has echoes in the practice of Bologna, a city governed for over forty years by a democratically elected Communist administration, which by the 1970s had essentially decided to deliberately arrest urban growth and architectural change in the name of a Communist approach to city planning.

Many cities in Europe and Asia (and a few in the Americas) have quite a long record, during the middle of the twentieth century, of creating spaces that weren't governed by speculation. The results are rather mixed. It would obviously be disingenuous to see the urban results as a slightly modified version of bourgeois practice, a sort of architectural "state capitalism." Typologies as different as the seven neo-baroque skyscrapers placed in a circle around the Moscow Kremlin at the end of the 1940s or the immense prefabricated housing estates of the 1970s are almost inconceivable without total nationalization of land and its conscious shaping in a certain historical interest. For sure it is not capitalist, and there is no way that any of this could have happened as a means of creating a surplus or profits for anybody. A quantitative difference, however, is distinct from the "qualitative" one Rossi speaks of.

What is absent everywhere in these situations is any conception of whether there is a difference between private property, state property and collective property, and whether or not that could have an effect on the architecture of the city. If democratically owned by an interventionist and collective polity, what would happen to the *locus,* and to the values of the historic city? Would it remain intact, as it did in Bologna, or would that transformation take more anarchic forms? And if it did, would it be recognizable as a city anymore?

IV The Thesis of Maurice Halbwachs

In the last twenty years Barcelona has become a top touristic destination. An important part of this achievement is due to the extensive effort in urban reshaping that started in the 1980s. The interventions in the historic center have played a key role in the regeneration and promotion of the city on the global stage. The operations in the Old City (Ciutat Vella), led by famous archi-tects like Bohigas and Busquets, were based on Aldo Rossi's theories on urban shapes, and followed an unusual dialogue between existing and new architecture. The creation of the whole new Rambla del Raval (1996–2001) through the demolition of almost 3000 houses in the historic tissue, has been the most consistent operation. The physical impact of the Rambla had been vast and deep: the transformations have gone way beyond the ex-pected effects, and one of the first consequences has been the creation of an ideal *terrain vague,* where the increasing communities of non-European immigrants filled both the physical and social voids created by the interventions. The "new" Old City of Barcelona entered into a process of gentrification, becoming an incre-dibly popular touristic destination, a result that exceeded any expectations when the renovation started. Newcomers (tourists, visitors and immigrants) have, quite obviously, adapted faster and better to the new morphology of the center and, differently from the locals, they appreciate the original historic features of old urban tissue.

Bureau A

Rambla del Raval, Bureau A, 2016

IV. Six Buildings on an Island or Planning for the Tropics

Who more sci-fi than us?
Junot Diaz, *The Brief Wondrous Life of Oscar Wao*

No longer painfully utopian, post-colonialism was reached as the last one was forced to leave. Unceasing decades of imposed regulations and internal corruption imploded the last hope of subsistence. The last years were the most intense ones. With warming temperatures extending the tropics beyond the limits of Capricorn and Cancer, a special unit of planners outlined the imminent destiny of the island once the entire population had been expropriated. A series of structures were erected. Some were the product of their immediate historical context. Others the result of a century of specialized intelligence.

For the first time in its history, the island witnessed precise planning. The territory was stripped of surplus modernization. Complete suburban structures disappeared, their concrete and steel crushed and collected by machines. Streets were unpaved, bridges dismounted. Automated drones surveilled aerially, looking for architectural debris. It took nearly a decade. The island was razed clean. There was no life left after colonialism, just architecture. Nature and architecture, to be exact.

Like neoliberalism, the "pill", and Agent Orange before it, the island became the test ground for new experiments. If the twentieth century raced to space, the frontier of the twenty-first century was in the tropics. The Warm War, as it was colloquially called, put hegemonic powers in technological confrontation once again. Direct attacks were out of the picture due to recent treaties. In exchange, proxy board games were deployed on key points around the globe. The tropics were pawns in a global chess match. Long held without any form of visionary innovation, the island finally followed the streams of the avant-garde. Six new archetypes were there future of the tropics. They were a manifesto of futuristic planning. It made the tropical island an experimental utopia.

Floating Fortress

The Floating Fortresses were the product of a carefully executed intelligence campaign that intercepted a plan making its way from Moscow to Cuba. Conceived in the 1920s by a cosmic architect, the Plan Krutikov consisted of floating architecture: a city hovering at consistent heights above the ground. After finding the secret plans, a group of architects specialized in speculative cosmonautics and quantum aeronautics concentrated on developing the project. Unable to move forward with the plans of building it due to impractical economic climate and slugging technological advancements, the Floating Fortress finally saw the light of day once Tropicalia was awarded governing autonomy. Scaled down and cast in ultralight concrete, the structure hosted a fortress to monitor the coasts of the island. A floating ring contained the supporting programs, while several watchtowers gathered and sent information to the communication posts on the shore. The Floating Fortress was equipped with an in-house prison system, detention and interrogation center.

Amphibian Fortress

Like a metallic star in a cosmic jungle, the Amphibian Fortress stood with its extended shiny, robotic limbs. Consisting of six rectangular members meeting on a common vortex, the Amphibian Fortress was able to move freely through any type of solid and semi-solid surface. The automated structure collected information on the island's soil, flora and fauna while sending waves to the communication structures on the island. The Amphibian Fortress gathered and distributed information about potential threats to the natural purity of the island. The Amphibian Fortress was a kinetic enforcer that, together with the Floating Fortress' ensured the island's security while protecting its tropicality.

WAI Architecture Think Tank: Cruz Garcia Nathalie Frankowski

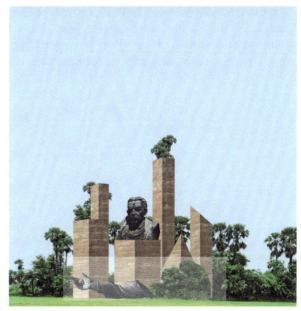

The Globe and the Javelin
Another prize of meticulous espionage, the plan for the Globe and the Javelin was captured during the years of the Cold War. Resting on top of mangroves, the Globe and the Javelin monitored weather conditions while receiving signals from the Floating and Amphibian Fortresses. Built with lightweight, self-regulating nano-fabrics, the Globe and the Javelin worked in combination. At night the globe floated free, lit with the rays deflected by the moon. On the mangrove, silently, the Javelin received and forwarded radio waves about the island and its surrounding sea.

Telescopic Towers
The Telescopic Towers were the largest structures erected since the island was reclaimed. Consisting of three towers anchored in the higher peaks of the central mountain range, the Telescopic Towers were connected by a series of hyper-sensitive fibers that created an informatics black hole (the world's most sensitive radio

wave receiver). Like Suprematist icons on the virgin landscape, the Telescopic Towers were the ears and brain of the agency in the mainland.

Aviary
The Aviary was in reality a detention center for tropical birds: a Guantanamo for colorful parrots. A lightweight structure assembled following simple geometric principles, the Aviary was first erected during the great Purge. Unsuspecting, the public thought of it as another zoological project, increasingly common during those days of political austerity and land acquisitions by the federal government. Birds thought to possess valuable information were detained, interrogated and studied in the Aviary. Some were taken from cages and trees. Others were snatched midflight. Highly sensitive sensors could detect both: birds flying thousands of kilometers away and beaks chewing on insects. In less than a year, no birds remained free. More Aviaries were spotted on the newly claimed landscape. Once tried with dolphins and rats, military training shifted its attention towards birds. Tropical birds were the new POWs. Those willing converted into allied spies. All birds sang. Some birds sang louder than the others.

Camp
Like nuclear no-go zones, the Camps were areas fencing in monuments, obelisks, effigies and icons of the life that used to occupy the island. During the years of the great purge, all forms of "historically significant architecture" (a concept officially employed to identify any form of subversive structure) were concentrated in these Camps. As the Camps were quickly filled, more Camps were built. The Camps were constructed on areas of transition, between the palm trees and the beach. The Camps were tropical museums: prisons for ideology, concentration camps for architecture.

134 Ⅳ Land Ownership

Cloé Gattigo

The Delhi Development Authority (DDA) was created in 1957 in order to cope with the influx of refugees which Delhi faced after the partition of India. This state-owned institution has been the single largest real estate developer in Delhi, leading land promotion, urban planning schemes or the development of housing typologies. This photograph is part of typological research conducted at the ETH Zurich, at the Studio Christ & Gantenbein, and was published in *Typology – Paris, Delhi, São Paulo, Athens* by Emanuel Christ, Victoria Easton, Christoph Gantenbein, Cloé Gattigo (Park Books, Zurich, 2015).

The Ordinary in the Problem of Housing

What follows in these few pages is a compilation of 24 floor plans of existing dwellings in apartment buildings in the city of Barcelona.

All of them with the north up, all at the same scale. Neither the name of the architect nor their precise location within the city are included. They are ordered by year of construction and incorporate their built-up area.

They have not been chosen or selected in any way.[1] They cover a period that goes from 1900 to 1992. This is not a conscious choice, but it nevertheless reflects a crucial period in the city, from the modernist era up to the celebration of the Olympic Games.

We often fixate on exemplary architecture. We study it, we visit it. Books are written about it. It is architecture that serves as a desirable model to follow. In doing this, we fail to acknowledge that most buildings that give form to the city are not exemplary.

What is common is necessarily never extraordinary. Even if sometimes the sum of ordinary parts can create an extraordinary whole.

If the city is largely characterized by collective housing, this collection of drawings offers an objective, though incomplete, portrait of the primary elements that form the city.

Each and every one is defined by its belonging to Barcelona, and each and every one contributes to the form of Barcelona. This intertwined relationship is a product of time and space; of the geographical, morphological, historical and economic aspects that define the city.

The City

In its origin, urban fabric can be either spontaneously created or rationally planned.

The city of Barcelona, geographically limited by the sea, the mountains and two rivers, is a dense ensemble of old quarters – highly compacted urban structures characterized by amorphous blocks and narrow streets – and the more recent expansions built in between and beyond, most notably the enlargement of the old center projected by Ildefons Cerdà.

Cerdà shares with Leonardo the aim to reach an ideal urban planning through the study of science, thus relegating it to the divine.[2]

In contraposition with the Gothic quarter, his proposal is based on a low-density non-hierarchical grid with its corners cut off, a 45-degree rotation from the north-south axis and the large size of its blocks, of 113m long per side. It is democratic in its homogeneity and forward-thinking in its communication system.

Not unlike the Paris of Haussmann, a project that precedes Cerdà's by only six years, it is a plan that represents a progressive impulse and an aim to improve the quality of housing and living in the wake of the industrialization of the city.

Cerdà's plan proves to be extremely rational in its organization, but has proven to be partly utopian in its realization, as the built volume nowadays quadruples what was originally intended. The result is a highly densified ensemble, not devoid of its own appeal, but which does not ultimately solve the housing problem by itself.

The City on the House

The city of Barcelona, whatever the area, is mainly formed by large enclosed blocks with buildings attached one to another. As a consequence of the relatively narrow land division, buildings become very deep, so as to occupy the maximum land possible.

To provide natural light and ventilation to these deep floorplans, small courtyards generally appear and service areas and secondary rooms gather around them. The climate and sun conditions of the city allow for this to function, but it also relates to the dominant Catholic morals of introversion, of hiding more than showing off.

Laura Bonell
Daniel López-Dòriga

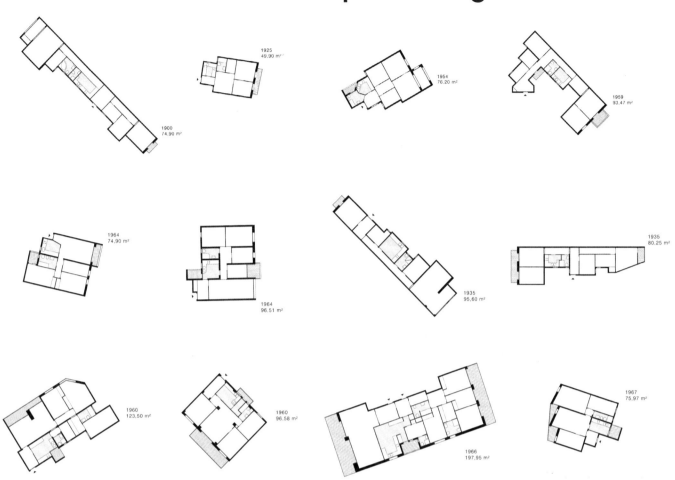

Three main dwelling typologies emerge:
1. Double-oriented apartments, with façades to both the street and the interior courtyard, often characterized by narrow layouts and long corridors.
2. Apartments with only one façade, either towards the street or to the inner courtyard.
3. Apartments in corner buildings, with two consecutive façades towards the street.

The House on the City
The morphology and particular attributes of these apartments have a direct impact on the form of the city.

Seventeen out of the 24 apartments were built between 1954 and 1979; none were built between 1936 and 1953. This is significant, as it directly relates to the history of the city and the country. In 1936 the Spanish Civil War started, which would go on until 1939. The climate of extreme poverty and uncertainty that followed was a direct cause of the low construction.

Only from 1953 on, with the end of the dictatorship's self-imposed autarchy and the arrival of international funds to the country, the economy started to grow and the shortage of housing was alleviated as construction works intensified. As a result, a great part of the city is defined by the architecture of those decades.

The practical absence of dwellings on the ground floors enables the occupation of these spaces with shops, bars, ateliers or garages, thus creating a decentralized urban fabric of mixed-use activities and lively streets.

The overwhelming presence of balconies adds a flair of customizable domesticity to the image of the city, otherwise defined by rationally structured façades, often load-bearing, with vertically proportioned windows. The balcony is an in-between space, the most public of all the private elements that conform an apartment in the collective housing and the expression of the individual self as part of the city, as seen by the proliferation of protest flags and banners, especially in the last few years.

The House

Taken out of their urban context, these drawings represent a miscellany of housing typologies. They epitomize the evolution of the housing typology in the twentieth century, or its lack thereof.

Despite the development of radical theories on the architecture of housing, most of them translated into reality at some point or another with various levels of success, we must conclude that in terms of the reality of where people live, this evolution is far from groundbreaking.

The city and its architecture are in constant change, while at the same time they evolve very slowly. Architecture is made to last, but it is at the same time a highly adaptable environment. We may live in one-hundred-year-old homes built in two-thousand-year-old cities, and still live in the present.

1   These drawings come from on-the-ground surveys done in the last year to complete a series of works regarding property valuation and various kinds of official certificates.
2   As it appears in the *General Theory of Urbanization* (1867) and "la Città Ideale" (1486).

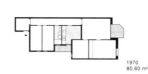

1978
91,20 m²

1984
113,05 m²

1970
80,60 m²

1970
79,70 m²

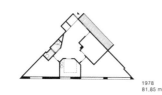

1976
81,09 m²

1978
81,85 m²

1991
124,50 m²

1992
117,50 m²

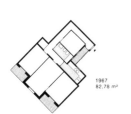

1967
82,78 m²

1968
61,09 m²

1971
77,69 m²

1974
75,65 m²

IV. The Architecture of the Territory?

Fifty years after *The Architecture of the City,* should architects consider the Architecture of the Territory?

In the mid-1960s, Rossi's book revolutionized ways in which architects engaged with urbanization. The megalopolis, the urban region and the levelling of differences between the city and the countryside were the characteristic urban phenomena of the period. Fifty years on, the scales of the urban have continued to magnify, and architectural tools for dealing with them have continued to erode. Rossi's text remains relevant; it sounds even truer today. Should, then, the scope of the discipline of architecture be broadened once again, beyond the limits of the city, to include urban territories? Do the scales of urbanization today demand a larger view?

(...)

Of course, territory is nothing new for architects. During the nineteenth and twentieth centuries, there is a history of architects' engagement with territory and urbanization: major modern architects have taken as a base of their projects extra-urban developments arising from industrialization and rural exodus.

This history has not yet been written, but many fragments exist. André Corboz, among others, in his text *La Suisse comme hyperville (Switzerland as Hypercity),* proposed that theories of urban design approached the problematic of urbanization in four distinct periods.

The first period, according to Corboz, aims to project "the city outside the existing city:" in 1859, Cerdà projected the urban fabric of Barcelona from the walls of the historical city outward to incorporate the neighboring villages. His seminal work was the 1867 book *Theory of Urbanization* – in fact, the term *urbanization* is credited to Cerdà.

Related projects dealing with urbanization in this period are Soria y Mata's Linear City from 1882, which organizes urban fabric along public transport lines, and Howard's Garden City from 1902, which aimed to create a network of small towns that would combine the advantages of both rural and urban living – a concept that has been realized over and over until today.

The second period in this development is marked by the Athens Charter, drafted in 1933. This is, confirms Corboz, an urban design theory "against the city" whose ideal is to replace the "unplanned" development of settlements, sometimes including historical ones, with socially, technically and hygienically "controlled" urban structures. In the same year, Walter Christaller proposed another highly influential theory, the Theory of Central Places. A Swiss example from this period is Armin Meili's *Landesplannung* (regional planning) from 1941.

What these theories had in common was a hierarchical vision of socio-spatial organization, anchored at the scale of national territory and corresponding to the Fordist organization of economy. However, while the theories argued for the complete control of urbanization processes under the patronage of the state, in practice, a major part of that responsibility was handed down to individuals – the atomized texture of private dwelling became a significant part of the fabric of the modern metropolis.

The third period of a backlash against excessive simplifications of the visions of the Modern, especially the reduction of the city to four basic functions, can be termed, Corboz suggests, "urban design within the city." It is based on *The Architecture of the City* as the key text, calling for the return to the idea of a city as a historical continuity. But architects in this period continued to see the territory as a theme of architecture, embracing the facts of urbanization beyond the canon. Proponents included Ungers, Koolhaas, Venturi and Scott Brown, Rowe, and so on.

Milica Topalovic

An exceptional project of the period dealing with territory is Cedric Price's Potteries Thinkbelt from 1964–66, concerned with reclaiming the derelict infrastructure of coal mining in the region of Manchester for the creation of a university – a visionary proposal for a new "knowledge economy" alternative to the declining post-industrial landscapes of Europe. The project was not realized, and the former mining area was returned to nature; today the site is a beautiful piece of wilderness (fig. 1 & 2)

The fourth period in this trajectory is ongoing, and its paradigm is still being negotiated. The defining condition is the merging of urban and territorial scale – in Corboz's words, "co-existence of city and territory." Many concepts have been coined to describe this condition, including *cittá diffusa, zwischenstadt* and *decentralized concentration.* Notable in this context is Andrea Branzi's Agronica – both a project

(fig. 1 & 2) Photographs: Bas Princen, from a series based on Cedric Price's Potteries Thinkbelt, Madeley Transfer Area site, Staffordshire, 2015. Perspective: Cedric Price, Potteries Thinkbelt, Madeley Transfer Area, 1964–66. Reproduction courtesy of CCA and B. Princen.

and a description of what he calls *weak urbanization,* horizontally spread across territory. Crucially for the territorial approach to urbanism, in this project Branzi expands the regular urban program to include agriculture and energy production.

In a groundbreaking analysis of contemporary urbanization entitled *Switzerland: An Urban Portrait,* in 2005 ETH Studio Basel put forward a thesis of Switzerland as a completely urbanized country. They showed urbanization putting pressure on the cellular structure of the Swiss commune and forcing the fabric of territory into new differences. The thesis also showed these differences as being no longer local, but increasingly integrated into the cross-border European context (fig. 3)

Along this trajectory of planning and designing urban territories and urbanization processes, in shifting from the period of Fordist economy – which emphasized the national scale – to the period of neoliberal globalization, the national territory has been abandoned as a relevant scale of planning, with some variations from country to country.

The national planning concept was replaced by a more flexible or provisional idea of strategic planning and by a focus on select strategic territories. Broadly speaking, urban areas or agglomerations today receive different amounts of attention in terms of investment and disinvestment. There is no specific relevant or fixed territorial scale; the scale or the frame is always contextual.

Linked to the same transformations is the changing position of architects among other relevant protagonists in urbanism and territorial or spatial planning. The new constellation foregrounds the role of engineers and engineering approaches as relevant to territorial planning, rather than the role of architects and urbanists. At the same time, as a consequence of these transformations, there is a shifting of the typical task of the architect into smaller spatial scales, from territory and city back to the building.

Looking at the examples I have mentioned, it is apparent that in different historical and political circumstances, the challenge of territorial urbanization has been a constant: territory was not a minor problem that has only recently gotten out of hand. The assumption that the late-twentieth-century city is ungovernable and unplannable, driven by laissez-faire politics, has given many architects an alibi for retreating into their strict professional mandate; but this is not any truer today than it was before. In fact, architects have continuously reinvented urban territories and the playing field of their practice. It follows that, as in all previous periods, architectural engagement with territory is still relevant and necessary.

What can architects today bring to territory and territorial scale? What should be our program?

Research beyond the boundaries of our discipline. I believe that in our discipline we do not have enough experience to tackle the problematic of urbanization alone. New interdisciplinary constellations should be built up – I believe that the link between architecture and urban geography is crucial.

Furthermore, an important means of engagement with landscape and territory comes through visual arts and through ethnographic practices – in keeping with Lucius Burckhardt's practice of walking, for example.

In this new constellation, there is an urgency of broadening the understanding of territory from the purely technical or administrative domain. Territory is a social and cultural fabric that architects are familiar with.

Design. Among other disciplines dealing with territory, architects' strength is design. Architects and urbanists have the advantage of synthetic thinking about territory beyond narrow specialization. Such synthesis is possible only through a qualitative and contextual approach.

Architecture and urbanism beyond the limits of the city. The idea is not new – throughout the twentieth century, the urban and the city have been elusive, unstable categories. For example, the recent concept of planetary urbanization theorised by Neil Brenner and Christian Schmid was helpful in reframing the urban problematic.

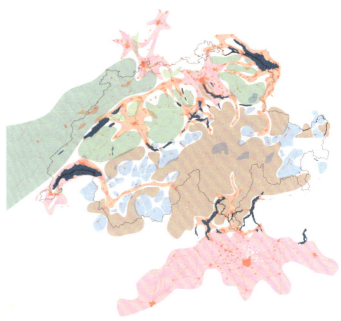

Once again, architecture and urbanism should extend their geographical field beyond the limits of the city to the research and design of urbanizing territories.

    Note: This is an edited excerpt of Milica Topalovic, "Architecture of Territory – Beyond the Limits of the City: Research and Design of Urbanizing Territories," lecture, presented at the ETH Zurich on November 30, 2015.

(fig. 3) Switzerland's urban potential: metropolitan regions, networks of cities, quiet zones, Alpine resorts and Alpine fallow lands. ETH Studio Basel, 2005. From: Roger Diener et al., *Switzerland: An Urban Portrait* (Basel: Birkhäuser, 2005).

IV Politics as Choice

"Politics as Choice" is the last chapter of *The Architecture of the City,* and perhaps it can be read as the summary of the entire book. What does "politics as choice" mean? *Who* choses *what?*

In order to answer these questions, it may be useful to understand the context in which Rossi wrote the book, originally published in 1966. *The Architecture of the City* was later translated and published in English in 1982, in the heyday of post-modernism. Rossi's iconic projects, such as the Teatro del Mondo, built as floating pavilion for the 1980 Venice architecture Biennale, provided the book with captivating images and references that contributed to make it a manifesto about the "autonomy of architecture." Yet the book was written in a radically different context as a polemical text within a specific debate that was important in Italy between the 1950s and 1960s.

This debate was about the issue of town planning and its effectiveness in governing the development of urban territories at the time of a strong economic growth. In that period, Italy experienced a sudden economic shift that in the span of few years changed the country's society from being mainly based on agriculture to increasingly relying on industry. This change had a massive impact on the Italian territory and on all aspects of social life. Large masses of people moved from the rural south to the industrial north. New infrastructures were built, such as a dense network of highways linking all the main centers of the long peninsula from north to south and from east to west. Cities were radically transformed with little concern for their rich historical heritage. With large masses of workers to be moved from rural to industrial production, the Italian government – led by the Christian Democrats with the support of the Socialist Party – embraced the welfare state. What happened in the US in the 1930s happened in Italy in the 1960s, the reorganization of the economic system by linking mass production with mass consumption.

The advent of the welfare state meant the radical industrialization of the territory far beyond the space of production towards the reform of all the aspects of social life: from housing to education from leisure to culture. It is at this point that town planning became a major concern for both politicians and architects. Until then, the Christian Democrats had maintained a weak control over urban development in order to favor the growth of the building industry as a lucrative but backyard system. Yet at the beginning of the 1960s such weak control was increasingly at odds with the pressure of industrial development. The necessity of town planning became more and more pressing, conferences were organized, books were published, and in 1962 the minister of public works launched a major urban reform that was boycotted by the same party to whom the minister belonged. The underlying assumption within all these events was that the city was no longer an *artifact,* but was an ever-changing organism in symbiosis with its surrounding region. Concepts such as city-region or city-territory were established as the new fulcrum of urban geography. Terms such as flows, links, networks and special economic zones were introduced into urban discourse for the first time.

In 1963, the Fondazione Olivetti organized a workshop to train young practitioners in town planning, led by three of the most important architects active in Italy: Ludovico Quaroni, Edoardo Detti and Gian Carlo de Carlo. Among the participants, acting as assistants, were Aldo Rossi and Manfredo Tafuri. While the latter was at that time busy with his collective AUA (architetti urbabisti associati) in studying the new urban phenomena such as the city-territory, Rossi launched a radical critique of town planning itself. It is possible to argue that it was precisely this occasion that inspired Rossi to write his book, and I believe that the last chapter condenses precisely the polemic that Rossi put forward during this seminal event.

Rossi's argument was directed against the way in which planning completely subsumed the scale of architecture as a concrete artifact, which for him was the only valid point for a project of the city. This polemic was mainly a critique towards the vague interdisciplinarity of town planning, yet it is possible to detect an implicit critique of the governance implied in planning itself. With planning, the city is reduced to the managerial logic of regulations and statistics. This approach is based on the assumption that political conflict and the possibility of decision (or choice, to use Rossi's term) is replaced by scientific parameters. Within the framework of town planning, the city becomes a natural product, the culmination of pure economic forces devoid of any political decision-making. Against this logic Rossi invoked *choice* as the moment that disrupts the assumption of the city as a natural product of progress. By choice Rossi means the moment of decision, the moment in which a community or an institution, by building or demolishing something, inevitably expresses a judgment on the city itself: "Who ultimately chooses the image of the city if not the city itself – and always and only through its political institutions."

In this statement, Rossi addresses institutions as the agents who make choices, and in this way he addresses a collective subject that is capable of political judgment. This is why Rossi is in agreement with thinkers such as Friedrich Engels, for whom the problem of the modern city was not its architecture but the political forces that produced it. Here Rossi assumed a position vis-à-vis the relationship between politics and architecture that is interestingly paradoxical. He sees architecture itself, a form, as something that alone cannot be *political*, yet he sees politics as something that in order to be tangible needs architecture.

For Rossi, architecture is a concrete means through which institutions can make their politics tangible. The city in all its concreteness and tangibility becomes the reification of these politics and allows those who confront those politics to accept or refuse them.

Paralela

Editorial
CARTHA

The core concept of Issue III is rooted in the exercise Roma Interrotta, from 1978, when Italian architect Piero Sartogo invited 12 architects to reimagine Rome by redrawing the Nolli map. For Lisboa Paralela, the current map of Lisbon will be used as a base, cutting out a section, running from south to north, across the city at its longest extent. A number of architects will be invited to redraw this section according to their visions of a possible parallel reality. The resulting drawing becomes an *acte manqué*, a representation of an alternative Lisbon.

The goal of this exercise is to display the unimpeded personal intentions of the invited architects: their visions of how the city of Lisbon could be. The architects are offered complete freedom to re-interpret the current city, both in physical and sociocultural terms. The concept of parallel reality is suggested both as a process to attain the goal and the goal itself, being that the resulting drawings will be depictions of parallel realities. The sole immediate consequence of this concept in the design process is that a parallel reality of any kind would inevitably be different from the one we find ourselves in. The degree of difference is for the architect to decide, ranging from altering the laws of physics, mirroring a neighborhood or tearing down/building a structure of some kind in the city. To reinforce the freedom offered to the architect in the exercise, the concept of *acte manqué* is suggested. If one would interpret the city as the result of the expression of society's conscience, one could ask how the city would be if there were no oppressive factors or entities, if a sort of continuous and conscious *acte manqué* could happen. What would the form of a city, that results from a different society with a different set of rules and expectations be?

The architect is free to invent his/hers own society in the exercise, in a subversion of Rossi's view on the role of the architect as a designer of "systems in which the spatial order becomes the order of society." Here, the architect is challenged to set his/her own "order of society" and therefore, the guidelines on how to approach the formal representation of their intentions.

When approaching the question of which map of the city should be used for the exercise of a parallel reality, it is clear that a depiction of the actual reality has to be offered as a base to envision alternative ones. The official DWG plan offered by the Lisbon Urban Department, unedited and unpolished, served as base for the architects interventions. Based on parallel realities, without social, political or natural restraints of any kind, the results show the unimpeded character of these architects and force us to look at Lisbon through their eyes, speculating on the present and, precisely because of that, perceiving it with renewed attention.

The remainder contributions to this issue, not limited by the geographic and chronographic constrains of 2016 Lisbon, broaden the scope and further load and inform the possibility of critically looking into alternative realities as a positive, constructive project methodology.

158	**Overview Map**
162 S1 227	**baukuh**

We believe that the Praça do Comercio is incomplete. It is missing a volume that could give back the urban tension to its void.

The new volume amounts to 33,675 square meters of easily marketable office space, distributed over five floors. Immediately west of the square, the elevation towards the Tagus is 288 meters long.

166 S2 228	**Edelaar Mosayebi Inderbitzin (EMI) Architekten**

Our map of central Lisbon does not represent a utopian notion of city, depicting instead the condition of today's city in a critical analysis. In a way, it depicts a contemporary image of the European core city in general. Over the course of various crises and the accelerated globalization of our economy and society, these cities are undergoing latent changes. In terms of its historical and cultural quality, the physical substance of the city is being reduced to containers that are refilled with globalized content. We read headlines of how vacancies are hollowing out the centers from within, how Airbnb is becoming the newest mode of gentrification, and how Asian buyers of property also get a European passport when purchasing a home. The permanence of the form (Rossi) shifts from the ground plan and the building type to the facade and the simple codes of so-called urbanity. The text of the city is rewritten, and the palimpsest of the urban fabric acquires yet another layer.

170 S3 232	**Camilo Rebelo**

All cities, like organic bodies, have problems. Structural design failures or bad postures can injury the system as a whole. These injuries tend to get worse with time, and when the system is already a living organism, destroying or demolishing is always an aggressive method to cure. Alternative ways to destruction should be considered.

Acupuncture is a technique that uses needles, sometimes associated with heat or small spheres being inserted into specific points of the body. It is an interventional procedure that strikes one point to heal an area.

On these premises we have identified seven cases in a sector of the city where we could use the acupuncture treatment. They reflect three types of intervention reinterpreted from this healing technique: punctual, gradual and temporary intervention.

174 S4 231	**MOS Architects**

Like most cities, it began with a grid, which made sense when we had to navigate, remember, negotiate and find our own way. Its single-mindedness physically structured all parts into a whole, providing orientation, location, address, memory and identity. It made things much more manageable and rational. We had a sense of where things stood in relation to each other.

What happened next is impossible to completely grasp. Maybe it was the landscape, maybe it was the people, or maybe no one was paying attention. But at some point cities grew unrepresentable as a totality, became an ungraspable, entropic mess of stuff and events – all the parts overwhelmed the whole. The city became a collection of monuments, of neighborhoods and archipelagos. We needed cognitive maps to make sense of it all.

Nowadays size and distance don't matter, only resolution. Objectivity is a matter of perspective. And everyone's sole concern is how strong their signal is. We are emancipated from everything. We are imprisoned by everything. We no longer need maps, cognitive or otherwise, only directions. We communicate in bed at any hour, with anyone, to anywhere; we collect friends; we search infinite heaps of information in an instant; we follow each other closely, from great distances: our memory and the navigation of cities are outsourced to the cloud. The city now fits neatly in our pocket, the unrepresentable chaos of the past now relatively manageable and representable. There are no differences between parts and wholes. Everything is simultaneously isolated and interconnected.

Open space for Lisbon, 2016

Studio Anne Holtrop

In our work we operate in an imagined architectural universe, a kind of ahistorical deep space in which works from all epochs meet on the same plain. Here, unexpected friendships are forged, coupling into surprising partnerships.

Lisboa Paralela is a city without monuments or memory. Its places bear the names of the 72 heteronyms that constitute Fernando Pessoa's literary universe, signifying nothing. In an equally hopeless effort, the architects propose a number of nameless structures that are modelled after some of their unbuilt designs. In a gesture full of optimism, we marry an architectural diptych with each of the eight sectors of the map.

Lütjens Padmanabhan Architekten
Eric Leo Gösswald
Oliver Lütjens
Thomas Padmanbhan

In an area planned to allow for walks, the interventions are clean breaks. Breaks in the pattern of the city and in the rhythm it provides. The courtyards introduce something both naive and excessive – a formalist simplicity that challenges the city.

As much as the entities serve to define public space, they are objects in their own right. And they share a simple, uncompromising language. The formal

Johannes Norlander Arkitektur AB

gestures are derived from a reworking and reduction of formal idioms – a plain architecture, like the one observed by George Kubler in the Portuguese tradition.

The forms emerge from the simplest gestures; the establishing of a wall, a roof or a floor. From this, a choreography is developed; through openings, flow, composition – and through references and relations to immediate surroundings. The result is an introspective urban object. Understood as a recurring typology, the entity suggests a city of narratives and intimate, irrational counternarratives. A city of promising tensions, and new kinds of shared experience.

The Alvalade district contains a verdant and diverse streetscape – most of it already present in the 1945 master plan, and later realized by various teams of architects, including a young Ribeiro Telles. Toward the airport, Alvalade becomes an aimless clash of interstitial and institutional space.

A seemingly missing element – in both the wide streets of the post-war plan and the confusion of the airport – are the dead ends of older cities; the courtyards of Nolli's Rome. In a parallel Alvalade, enclosed spaces appear at key points. Inserted into the flowing master plan, freestanding courtyards add tension to their surroundings. Next to the airport, a wall is opened, and an outdoor pool stretches into the landscape. These are pure objects, containing intimate public space. Clearly defined, and still ambiguous, the entities suggest a city with different levels of shared life.

Raphael Zuber

The "city of common space" defines the public space, leaving the maximum degree of freedom for the privately owned parts.

Infrastructure is rationally organized in an orthogonal grid. Streets and squares are given profiles and are freely distributed, creating one continuous, designed space throughout the whole city.

The only urban rule for private construction is to build a wall as part of the common space, acting as a façade for each single building and the entire city at the same time. The wall can be freestanding or attached to a construction behind it and can have a certain percentage of openings. Buying a plot, one would have to choose, for example, between a wide street with a low wall or a narrow street with a high wall bending over the sidewalk.

The conflict between the precisely predefined and the self-regulated, as well as the ambivalence between uniformity and the unpredictable beauty of chaos, will determine the physical expression of the city and generate a highly mixed and inventive environment.

A dusty path, just recognizable among the shrubs and tumbleweeds dotting the foothills of the mountain range, provides just enough room to guide a horse. The desert path, coming in and out of view, winds its way over and between these hills making its way somewhere, meandering as it goes. The path eventually leads to a place, in this case to a long-stripped valley, which appears below the foothills. A small town appears along this valley, its buildings showing enough affinity for each other to provide the town with a barely monumental presence in the otherwise desolate environment. The path moves past the town's sign announcing its city limit, but as the rider approaches the entrance of the town the path begins to fade into a street-like landscape. Facing buildings provide the only structure needed for defining the street, which would otherwise just be a dusty, shrubby, rattlesnake-ridden and infinitely expanding ground plane. There is no structure known as infrastructure here and if there is, it happens automatically, as a casual yet legible by-product, never conditioning yet always being conditioned.

(194) (S10)
(227) Ciriacidis Lehnerer Architekten

(196) Nothing is More Abstract than Reality: The Current State of Affairs
(227) Patrícia Barbas

(198) Poliorceticon,
(226) Babau Bureau:
Stefano Tornieri
Massimo Triches
Chiara Davino
the Form of the Siege

(202) How Tourism is Reshaping Urban Realities
(233) Daniela Silva

Metropolis

204 Rome: A Borderline
230 Labics:
Maria Claudia Clemente
Francesco Isidori

210 Domestic Forms
229 Simona Ferrari

216 Invisible Infrastructures and Their Forms
231 George Papam Papamattheakis
231 George Foufas

220 Time Catalyst Forms
226 Pau Bajet

222 In-Formed Lisbon
231 Pedro Pitarch

The goal of the *Lisboa Paralela* exercise is to display the unimpeded personal intentions of the invited architects: their visions of how the city of Lisbon could be. The architects are offered complete freedom to reinterpret the current city, both in physical and sociocultural terms. The concept of parallel reality is suggested both as a process to attain the goal and the goal itself, being that the resulting drawings will be depictions of parallel realities. The resulting drawing becomes an *acte manqué,* a representation of an alternative Lisbon.

A section of a current map of Lisbon running along the north-south axis of the city is subdivided into 10 equal parts, each of which is offered to an architect as a site to be reimagined. The particular choice of this strip of city is neither random nor innocent; its intention is to dissect the chronologic and geographic layers of the city, from its genesis (as a medieval castle) and lowest point (Mouraria) to the twenty-first-century political borders and highest point of Lisbon (Airport). The remaining city is off limits. Although the architects are given carte blanche to manipulate and curate the city within the stripe, the imaginary lines that delimitate these zones are absolute borders that cannot be crossed. Based on parallel realities, without social, political or natural restrains of any kind, the results show the unimpeded character of these architects and force us to look at Lisbon through their eyes, speculating on the present and, precisely because of that, perceiving it with renewed attention.

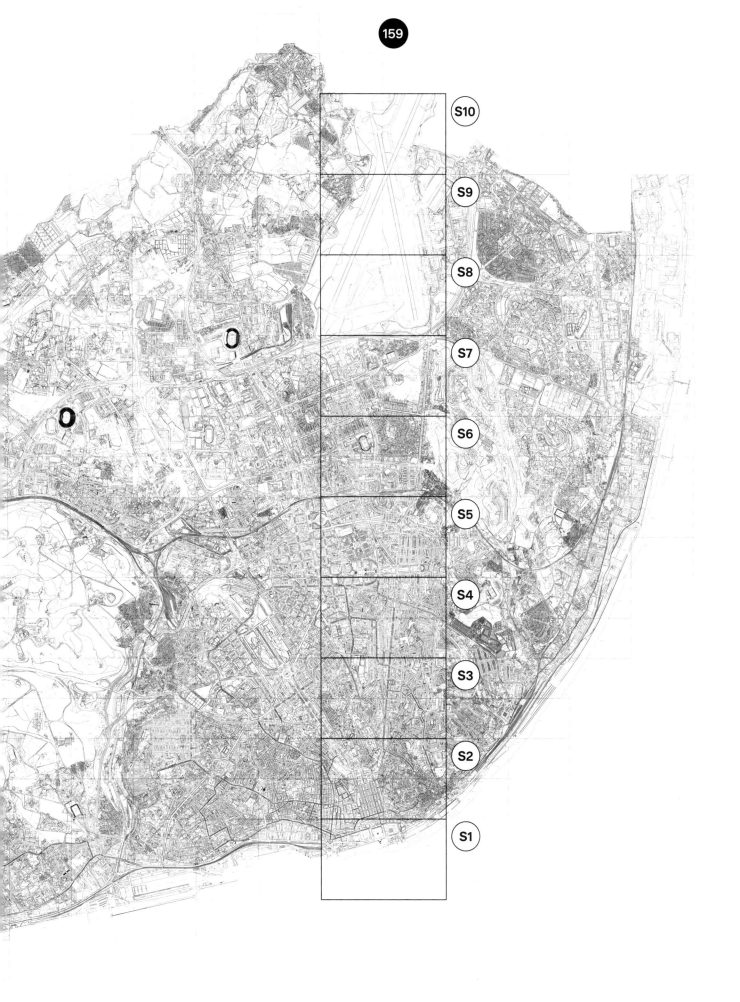

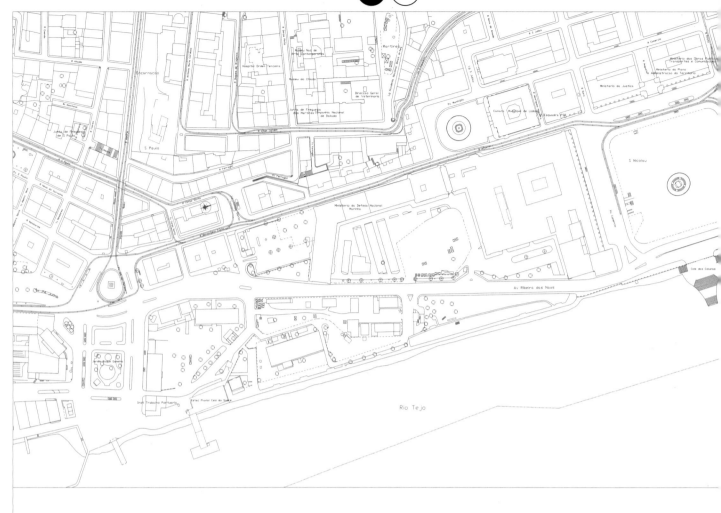

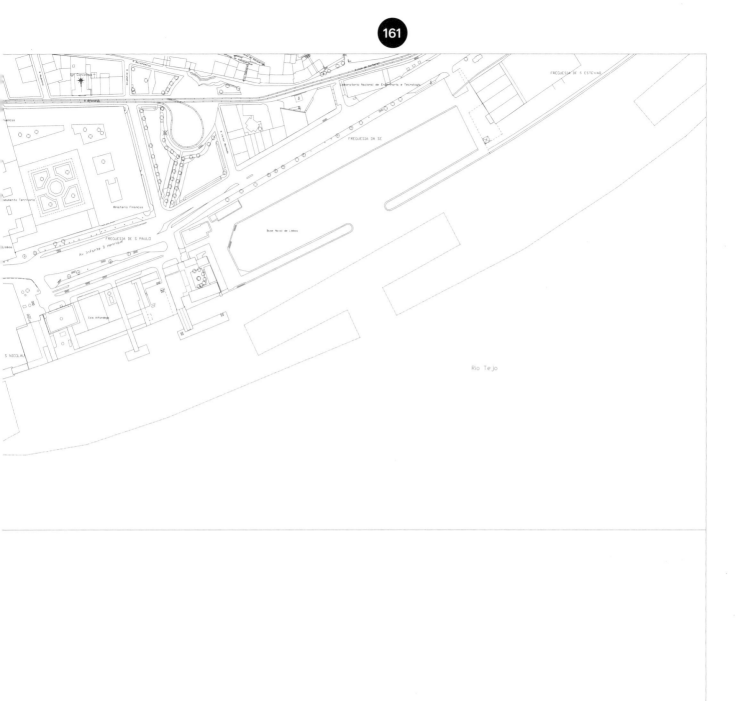

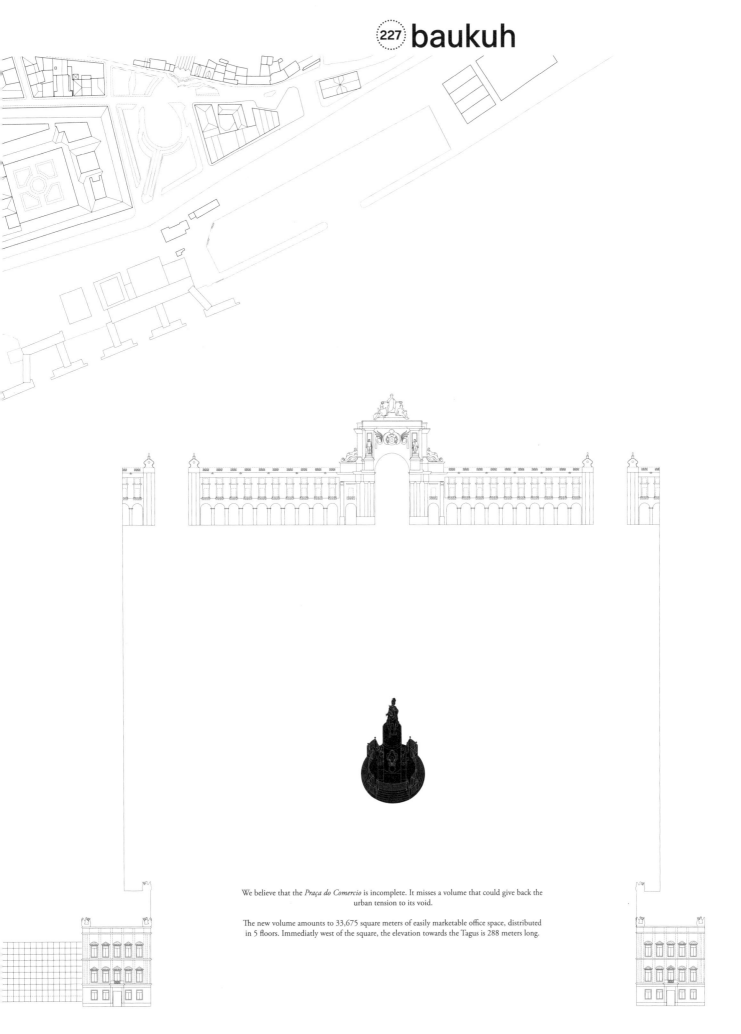

We believe that the *Praça do Comercio* is incomplete. It misses a volume that could give back the urban tension to its void.

The new volume amounts to 33,675 square meters of easily marketable office space, distributed in 5 floors. Immediatly west of the square, the elevation towards the Tagus is 288 meters long.

228 EMI Architekten

OVERWRITING THE EUROPEAN CITY
Edelaar Mosayebi Inderbitzin Architekten
1:2000

Our map of central Lisbon does not represent a utopian notion of city, depicting instead the condition of today's city in a critical analysis. In a way, it depicts a contemporary image of the European core city in general. Over the course of various crises and the accelerated globalization of our economy and society, these cities are undergoing latent changes. In terms of its historical and cultural quality, the physical substance of the city is being reduced to containers that are refilled with globalized content. We read headlines of how vacancies are hollowing out the centres from within, how Airbnb is becoming the newest mode of gentrification, and how Asian buyers of property also get a European passport when purchasing a home. The permanence of the form (Rossi) shifts from the ground plan and the building type to the facade and the simple codes of so-called urbanity. The text of the city is rewritten, and the palimpsest of the urban fabric acquires yet another layer.

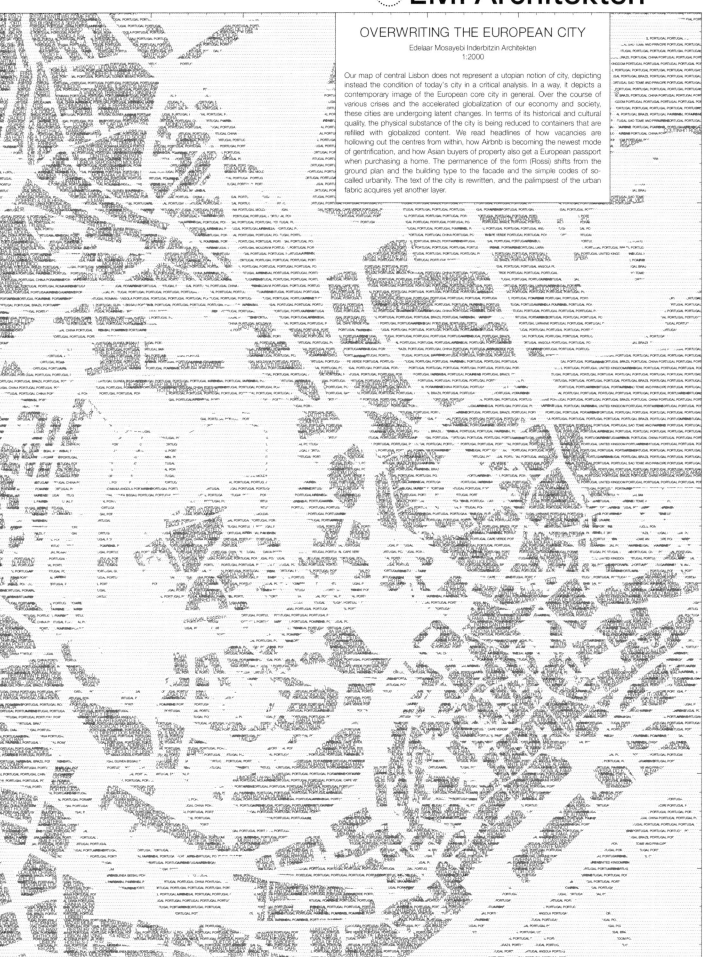

Camilo Rebelo

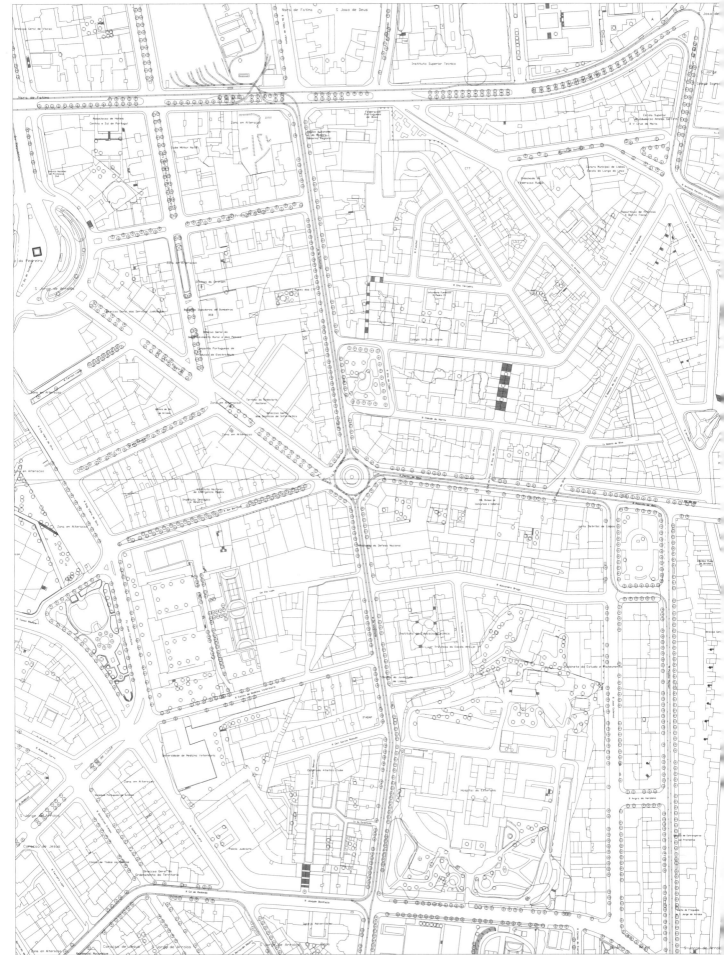

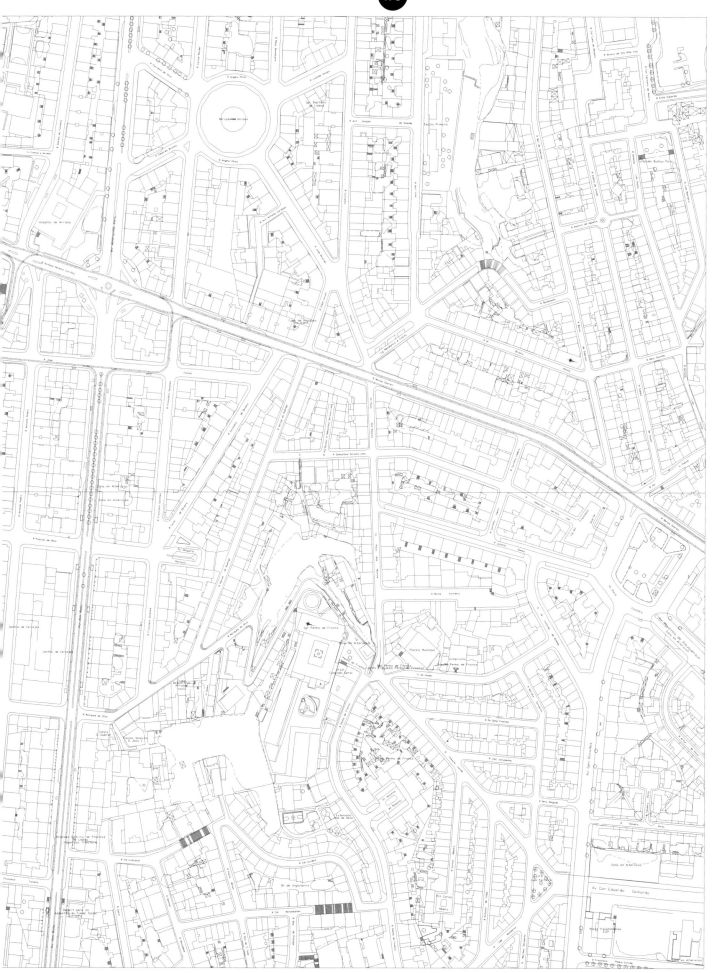

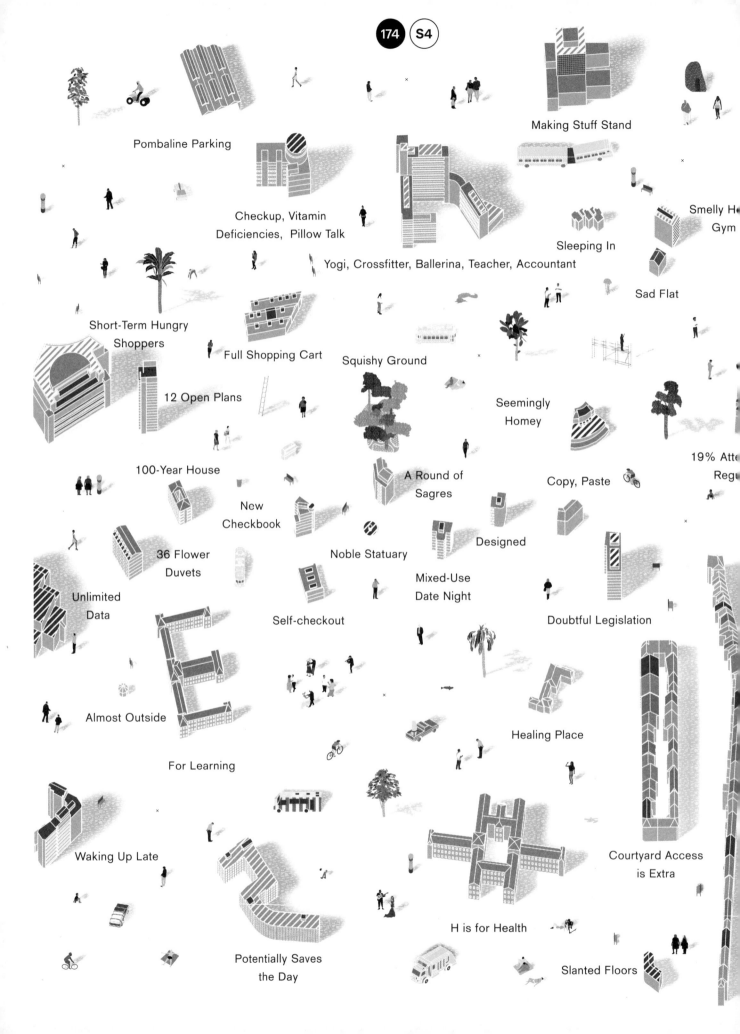

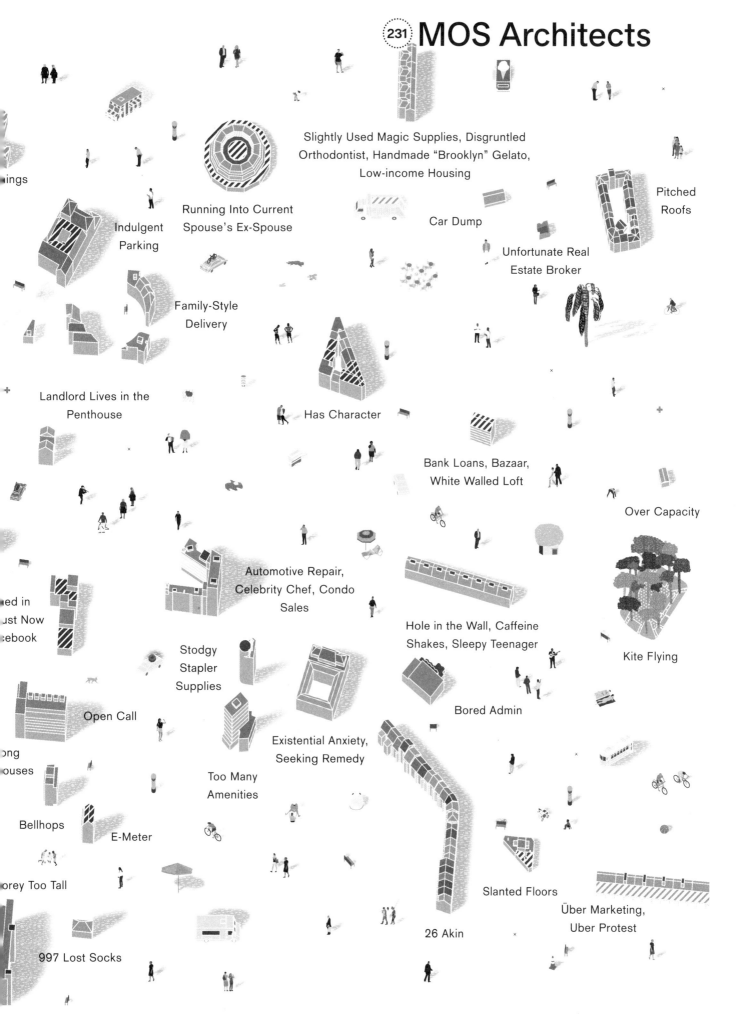

229 Studio Anne Holtrop

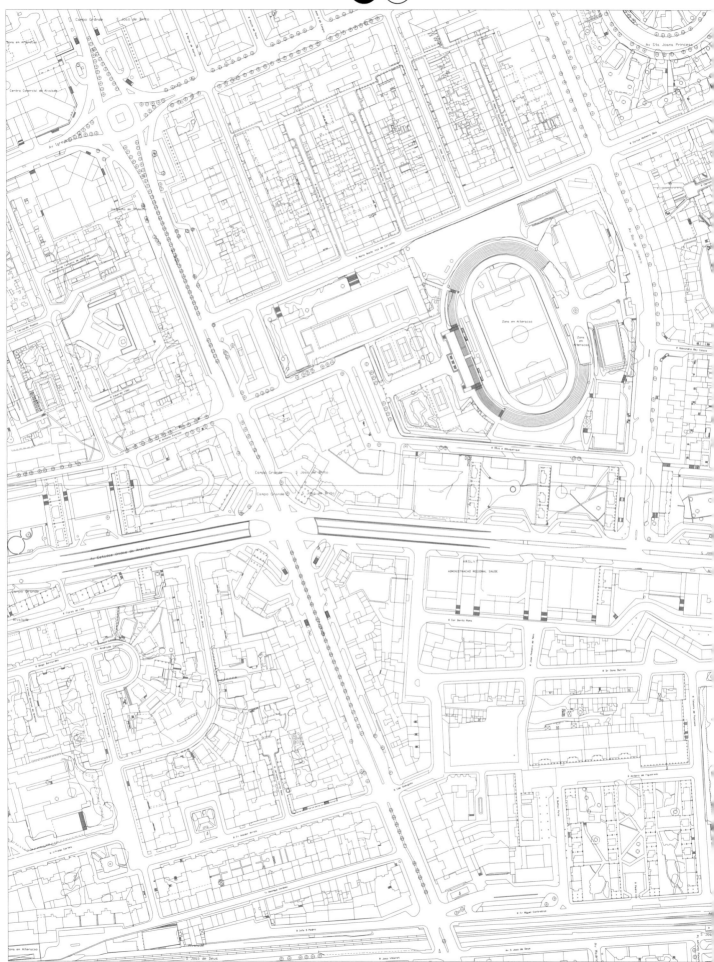

Lütjens Padmanabhan Architekten

184 S7

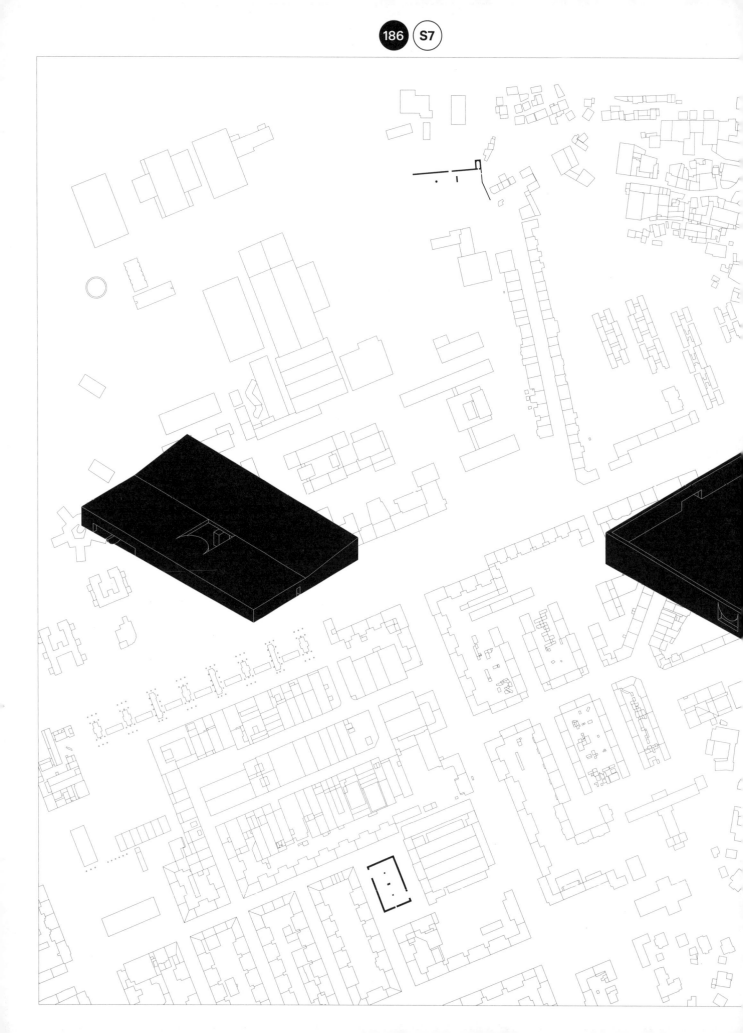

231 Johannes Norlander

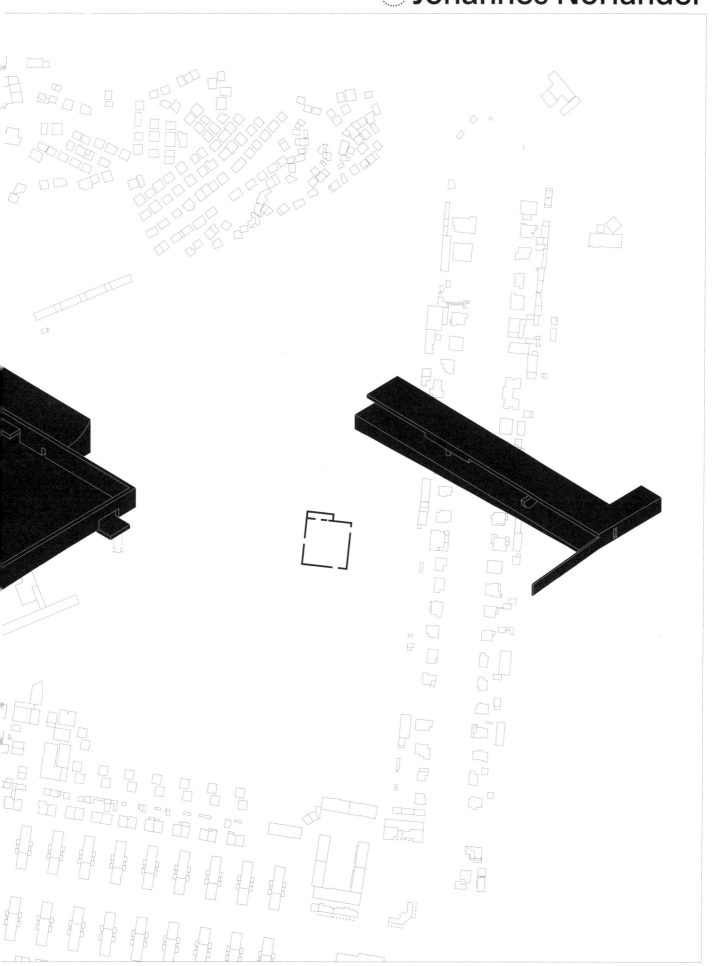

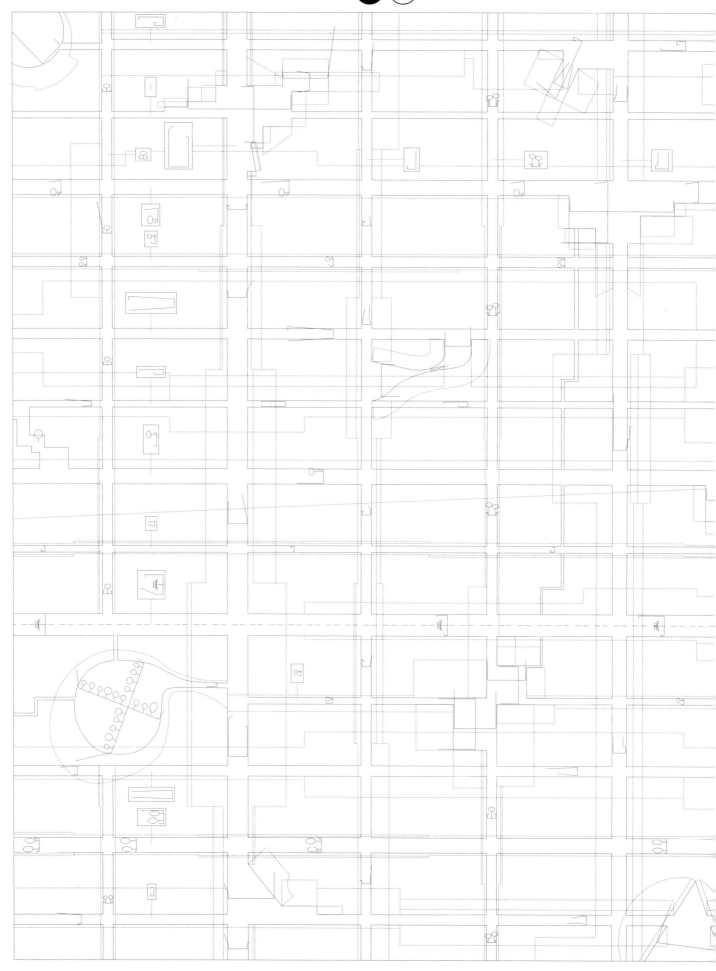

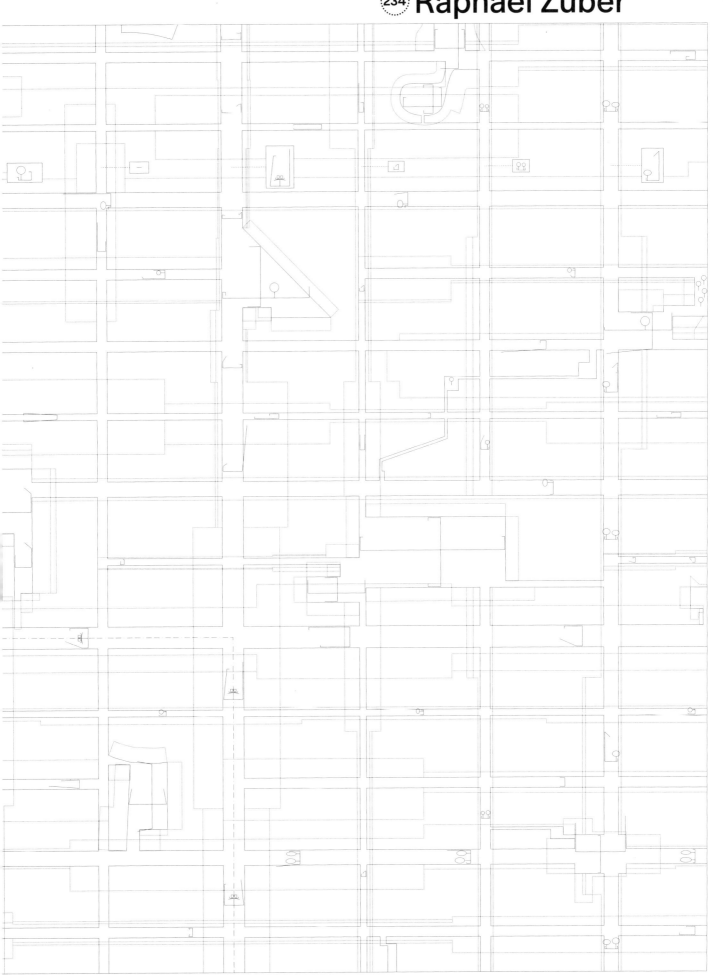

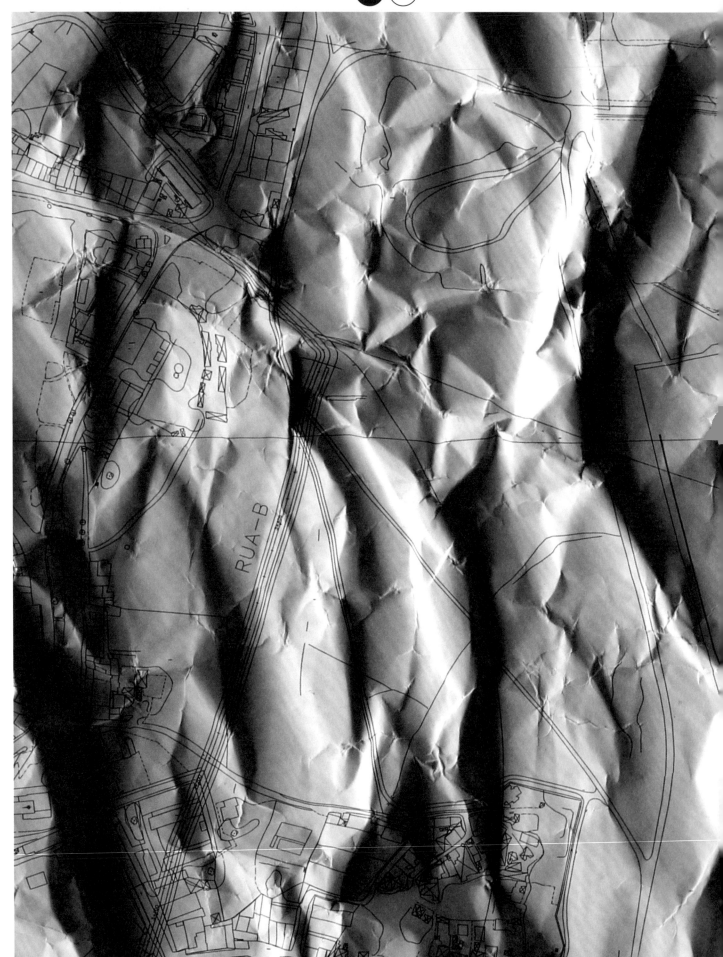

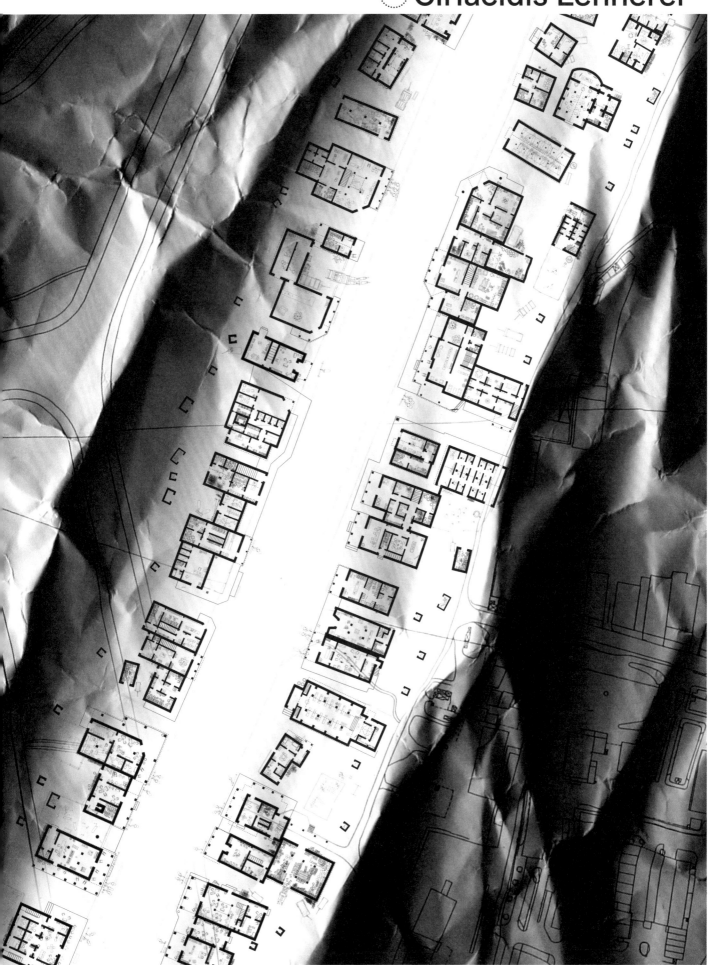

227 Ciriacidis Lehnerer

Nothing is more Abstract than Reality: The Current State of Affairs

Instead of utilizing the circulated draft, I rather prefer to share my thoughts, which I assume are shared by a sizeable portion of my generation, on what is the current state of affairs. And I'm thinking about a current perspective on the discipline and on our lives as well, because I cannot conceive of being an architect without a strong awareness of the world in which I live. And as long as I'm around I will do my best to hold onto the idea that we must contribute to the construction of a better world, conducting both my professional practice and my life according to the these principles, which I was fortunate enough to inherit from my parents and which I find everyday in my family, friends, colleagues and students.

In this present world, a character like Donald Trump can think about winning a presidential election in the United States. The release of the Panama Papers can bring down the Icelandic government the day after. The Europe in which we live is plagued with inequality; the acronym coined to group the countries in economic crisis could hardly be more demeaning: PIIGS; and the Greek situation confirms the widening of the fracture between North and South. The European Union in which we live is once again putting up walls, like in Hungary, blocking the entrance to refugees running away from war torn countries, and watching daily, with unruffled indifference, the deaths of thousands of people trying to cross the Mediterranean. The apparent stability is over. *Nothing is more abstract than reality.*

We are the generation who witnessed both the inception and the failure of the ideals of the European Union: the fall of the Berlin Wall, the opening of the Schengen space, free circulation of people and goods, ease of access to information and fast communication, Wi-Fi, social networks and low-cost flights. We are the generation who watched the prodigality with which European funds were wasted, who watched both the rise of the credit bubble with easy money and its burst, the rise of coruuption – and the generation who will still be around to pay the bill. We are also the generation who fought against the rise of tuition, who fought for our rights and who demonstrated against social and political injustice. We are the ones who felt the loss of identity, the indignity and shame when our countries sold their souls trying to become part of the first league – the Northern one, of course. No, we are not all the same. Nothing is more abstract than reality.

We are the more travelled generation, with friendships across the world and a lived perspective from other realities. We are the ones who emigrated looking for work, and the ones who choose to stay in our countries despite the difficulties. We believe that we can do better, try better and fail better. We are the true embodiment of the word sustainability. We agree, with the same commitment, to refurbish a cousin's kitchen, to write a text, to design exhibitions, cities, or real and unreal buildings, and we do not feel lesser for that. We use the lack of opportunities to bundle efforts, to make alliances, to think collectively, to write and mobilize. We are not pampered children and do not need patronizing. We demand parity; we demand to be treated like peers. We rebel and do not fear the heated debate necessary to understand our time, despite the extreme confusion of the present.

Patrícia Barbas

This was a letter to the president of the FAD 2016 jury, written as a member of it and sent in May 2016. It was based on a draft, made by him to be commented and completed as the result of all our conversations and debates. In our first jury meeting, I was classified as a "young architect" despite my 45 years. In the draft, he used such key words as "crisis", "never-ending recession", "new paradigm", "sustainability" and "European convergence in a way that I could not disagree with more. I decided to publish here "because this applies to a much larger audience. Unfortunately, Moises Gallego is not alone, and because of that, this is a statement of a generation that speaks not only for itself but for the ones younger than us, already out there with all capabilities and in defiance of beginning and enduring life and practice. We will not go down as the ones who undermine our youngest; who, like Kronos devoured our sons to prevent to being overcome by them. We are the present, the caretakers of the future of our discipline.

Poliorceticon, the Form of the Siege

> […] crusaders are going to Not assist Portuguese to conquer Lisbon, it is written and so it is the truth, even if different, what we called false prevailed over what we call true, it took his place, someone could come and tell the new story […].[1]

Raimundo Silva, a lowly proofreader for a Lisbon publishing house, by inserting a negative into a sentence of a historical text, alters the whole course of the 1147 siege of Lisbon. The past and the reality can be rewritten as a romance, a pure invention that sometimes becomes history. The example of the siege, as a theoretical background, suggests in this case a method for the design processes of a city. The ideal city has to be imagined; the real city has to be conquered.

Poliorceticon is a permanent process that involves transformative heterogeneous and punctual actions in the territory in order to provoke systemic reactions and relations between the parts of the contemporary city. Poliorcetics is the branch of military art that studies methods, techniques and means for besieging cities and fortresses. It is an art that, like architecture, transforms places into tools, actions and strategies and implies a strong knowledge of subjects that go beyond the *Art of War* and include engineering, geology, anthropology and politics.

The idea of conquest is not just linked to control, supremacy and suppression, but also to fusion among cultures, as in the case of Alexander the Great and the fusion of his Hellenic Reign with native peoples. Taking these considerations into account, the contemporary territory can be read as a juxtaposition of antithetical city models, and its form as the synthesis of different interpretive and modelling capacities typical of men and of their being-in-the-world.[2] The contemporary city is characterized by the coexistence of profoundly different types of city models.

Imagining future scenes in order to understand such a complex territory, means starting from a transformative process project, thought up not necessarily to be connected one with the other. On such a theoretical basis, the project proposal interprets the theme of physical reconquest of places and the possibility for the community to regain collective knowledge of the territory where it lives through the modification tools used in architecture. The imaginary scene regards the near future and considers the present city as the reality from which to start. Through different punctual interventions, the first step for the reconquest of the contemporary city takes place through new connections among existing elements, able to build a renewed accessibility, with the scope of creating porosity and functional connections.

Some of these areas, once transformed, will be available for the spontaneous and temporary utilization of their inhabitants. The "conquest" process will be considered finished only when a series of new interventions form with the pre-existing a total functional urban mix, configuring itself as a "city without plan."[3] This is a city model built on fragments that derive from pieces put side by side for addition, from the repetition of independent elements, from "out-of-sync" buildings, and combined with no logic, but which will be a fusion between productive and living culture.

Tools of Siege

A siege starts with strategic actions such as the identification of the weaknesses of the city to be conquered. Walls, canals, structures, fences, infrastructures, elements that constitute interruptions, limits, critical points, the trespassing of which is the first action of breach and entrance to the besieged city. Poliorecetics ensures that city boundaries can be attacked, to start the conquest process, using devices, machines or siege tools. Connective tools able to open breaches, small architectures that trespass limits that today cannot be solved, demolition of defensive barriers witnessing an industrial past; the art of poliorcetics serves for the transformation of a territory that must slowly be reconquered by the people.

Babau Bureau:
Stefano Tornieri
Massimo Triches
Chiara Davino

Camps
A second phase of the siege foresees that the customs and part of the changes of the territory derive from non-planned and non-regulated methods. The spontaneous birth of new uses of the spaces will cause the temporary movement of the control of the urban changes from government institutions to the people. It is expected that the spaces accessible and available shall be repopulated, used, and modified by their spontaneous utilization. Eventually, the relationship between territorial and social changes implied in such actions will be studied in consideration of its central role in the understanding of the socioeconomic changes of the area. The bottom-up approach used in this phase is intended as an indicator of changes that now, for the rapidity and complexity with which the context conditions change, would be impossible to foresee by a territorial planning project.

Conquests
It is impossible to foresee the future form of the city because a lot of stakeholders are involved in its transformation. Strategies could be enhanced, in order to develop conquest methods specific to places, in which the architect will act as a strategist. In the future city, production landscapes such as industries or quarries, infrastructures, shopping spaces and wastelands will coexist peacefully with the living culture. New buildings will stand among silos and chimneys, but synergetic processes of production and energy transmission will investigate visions of a possible autocracy. Reclaimed land, in this sense, is intended as the conclusion of the reconquest

process of a territory, as the total sum of energy able to build a systematic principle that generates changes in the territory.

Every intervention shall use local resources in order to present itself as a conscious model for future developments.

History of the Siege

Living in a place also means having a kind of narrative heritage made of a plurality of mental images, sometimes measurable, perceptible. As sensed by J.E. Hobsbawn in *The Invention of Tradition,* every society has accumulated a reserve of apparently ancient material, often merely invented, to legitimate and build their roots.

For this reason, the project also uses a tale, a short story, the interpretation of which significantly contributes to the perception of the places, to people's feeling at home in such places, creating a sort of mental projection. Places become occasions to set stories, to build mental images necessary to the construction of the feeling of belonging to a place.

> [...] the problem I have to solve is different, when I wrote Not the crusaders
> went away, therefore my looking for an answer to the question is
> pointless, Why in this history accepted as being true, must I myself invent
> another history so that it might be false and false so that it may be different.
> [...] He realised that until he overcame the problem he would make
> no progress, and was surprised, accustomed as he was to books in which
> everything seemed fluent and spontaneous, almost essential, not because
> it was effectively true, but became any piece of writing, good or bad,
> always ends up appearing like a predetermined crystallization, although no
> one can ever say how or when or why or by whom, he was surprised,
> as we said, for the following idea had never occurred to him, an idea which
> should have stemmed naturally from the previous idea, but on the contrary,
> refused to emerge, or perhaps not even that, it simply was not there,
> did not exist even as a possibility.[4]

1 Josè Saramago, História do cerco de Lisboa. (History of the siege of Lisbon), 1st ed. Caminho, Lisbon, 1989. English edition edited by Houghton Mifflin Harcourt, 1998.
2 Martin Heidegger, *Sein und Zeit,* Halle, 1927.
3 Daniel Libeskind, *City without plan,* Blau, 1992.
4 Josè Saramago, Ibidem.

How Tourism is reshaping Urban Realities

Following the loss of heavy, manufacturing industry in many industrial areas in the 70s and 80s, tourism has featured extensively in urban and waterfront regeneration policy because of its ability to generate substantial economic benefits to destination communities. This, alongside a number of additional facts, has created a flux of mass tourism to certain cities, in which Lisbon is included. Mass tourism has created a parallel reality within cities and developed a very complex relationship to cities' urban forms. But before we can discuss these relations, I would like to shed some light on the concepts of tourism and urbanity.

To be a tourist is one of the characteristics of the modern experience, for it is modern society that has provided the enabling factors for people to travel and for the supply of tourism destinations, services and amenities. Indeed, for the majority of people living in developed countries, tourism is feasible. Due to technological advancements, mass transportation, the provision of leisure time and increasingly high levels of disposable income, people now have the means and opportunity to travel and explore different places. Additionally, few places in the world today have not become either tourist destinations or in close proximity to them, and the overall number of people participating in tourism continues to grow. Thus, the demand for travel has increased and the supply of tourist destinations, attractions and facilities has also distended to correspond with demand. In the past thirty years there has been a fundamental shift in consumption habits, including the consumption of holidays. No longer do we asprive for package beach hotel holidays but rather, these traditional holidays are being rejected for individualistic, personalized forms of tourism – for example, urban tourism (including short/city breaks), eco-tourism and heritage tourism. Consequently, new tourism destinations have emerged, such as urban waterfront destinations like Lisbon.

Globalization can be characterized as the increasing connections (social, cultural and economic) that are taking place around the world. What is in effect happening in today's society is a wave of cultural transformation associated with a process of cultural globalization. As cultural products such as tourism are assembled from all over the world, they are turned into commodities for a new global marketplace. Thus, as cultures are thrown into immediate contact with each other, new geographies are formed with an emphasis upon the renaissance of locality. For instance, places attempt to revitalize the local as local cultures are overshadowed by a new global culture. Arguably, this new spatial aesthetic reflects postmodern culture with its emphasis on local and vernacular cultures, while its global orientation tends to produce a new certainty in which place distinctiveness is etched out for the sake of achieving universally accepted standards of the cultural economy.

As international relations multiply and localities become similar to one another, such a loss finds its cultural expression in the theme of nostalgia: "A movement towards one's roots and a growing appreciation of tradition are aspects of relating to one's total environment. They reflect the interplay between the local and the global. Such trends can be viewed as manifestations of postmodernism."[1] During the postmodern era, in areas where manufacturing industries have diminished and deindustrialization has occurred, as is the case of Lisbon, desolate sites have been redeveloped and reinstated with the injection of service industries and consumer-based activities. These new sites cater as tourist centers, where heritage and other forms of tourism have been used to transform the landscape. Spaces such as these embrace a postmodern orientation and arguably appeal to the lifestyle choices and consumption ethic of the new middle class. The creation of the new middle class is responsible for the gentrification of such areas and is connected to the growth of such developments. The phenomenon of waterfront redevelopment is a highly visible example of contemporary urban restructuring. In many cities, efforts have been made and are currently being made to renew the strengths of the waterfront through large-scale renewal projects.

These changes dramatically alter the original character and function of the port area from a site of production to a cultural landscape more readily associated with consumption practices. Perhaps one of the most striking characteristics of regenerated dockland vicinities is their distinctive postmodern appearance and appeal. For example, Dodson and Kilian[2] argue that processes of commodification and "spectacle-isation" have been used to redevelop and forge "post-modern" waterfront destinations.

According to Law[3] "the term urban tourism simply denotes tourism in urban areas". Shaw and Williams[4] state that urban areas of all types act as tourism destinations and these areas have the potential to attract domestic and international tourists. They argue that tourism in these environments is a diverse phenomenon. First, urban areas are heterogeneous in nature as they are distinguished by size, location, function and age. Second, they are multifunctional as they offer a variety of facilities. Third, facilities are consumed by a whole range of users – for example, tourists and residents. Cities provide a great range of consumption opportunities for users. These and the facilities to supply their needs define a range of different types of city which may all exist within a particular urban area – for example, the shopping city and the historic city. For Law, it is difficult to define urban tourism due to its diversity, however, his attempts at describing the phenomenon of urban tourism have primarily focused on its demand and supply-side characteristics, which enable the subject to be differentiated from other types of tourism.

Over the last three decades, tourism has had an important role in the regeneration of urban areas in Lisbon. It has contributed to urban revitalization with the recovery of old buildings and by bolstering the country's economy. The historic center of Lisbon experienced a negative development in its physical, social and economic conditions throughout the twentieth century. The problem of urban decline is related to a set of heterogeneous and interacting factors such as suburban sprawl and the freezing of rents (depriving landlords of the incentive to maintain properties and rehabilitate housing).[5] The process of decline in historic city centers has been inseparable from the decline in the resident population.

The money tourists spent helps Portugal's economy, and the government heralded the flood of tourists as a sign that Lisbon is the place to be. For some residents, however, such flows risk ousting local inhabitants and traditional stores from the city's ancient quarters as hostels and shops selling cheap trinkets and imitation handicrafts encroach. The changes are most evident in the Baixa area, a grid of black and white cobblestone streets between two hills facing the River Tagus. An area once dominated by local boutiques has faced an influx of low-budget hotels, restaurants with menus in multiple languages and souvenir shops hawking cheap Portuguese-style products made in China. This new city center came as a response to the problems of degradation, loss of resident population, and ageing of vacant buildings that the city was suffering. What happens when everything around you turns into shops selling souvenirs? Tourists who come to Lisbon will no longer be able to see the best of what we have to offer.

Lisbon, as many other cities transformed by the mass of tourism, now has a parallel reality, where the locals have one kind of experience and the tourists are led to believe in a different kind of city, a fabricated city for them to enjoy.

1   Nuryanti, W. (1996) "Heritage and postmodern tourism," *Annals of Tourism Research*, Vol. 23, No. 2, pp. 249–260.
2   Dodson, B. and Kilian, D. (1998) "From Port to Playground: The Redevelopment of the Victoria and Alfred Waterfront, Cape Town," in D. Tyler, Y. Guerrier and M. Robertson (eds.), *Managing Tourism in Cities: Policy, Process and Practice,* England: John Wiley & Sons.
3   Law, C. M. (2002) *Urban Tourism: The Visitor Economy and the Growth of Large Cities,* London: Continuum.
4   Shaw, G. and Williams, A. M. (1994) *Critical Issues in Tourism: A Geographical Perspective,* Oxford: Blackwell.
5   Alves S. (2010) *O Social, o Espacial e o Político na Pobreza e na Exclusão – Avaliação de iniciativas de regeneração de áreas urbanas 'em risco' na cidade do Porto.* PhD Thesis, Instituto Superior de Ciências Sociais, Lisbon University, Portugal.

Rome: A Borderline Metropolis

Foreword
The image of Rome narrated by a distracted traveler at the beginning of the nineteenth century or the image absorbed by the thousands of tourists that every day invade the city has remained substantially the same. In the collective imaginary, Rome is always itself: The Eternal City.

But can this image represent the true nature of the city and above all, that of contemporary Rome? Would it be possible to find a new mental image able to represent the entire city and its complexity?

Borderline metropolis[1] is an attempt to answer those questions and at the same time is an investigation of the territory of Rome as well as a study that offers a different interpretation of the contemporary city.

Phenomenology of a City – A View from Inside
The investigation began with a true urban phenomenology, with a *bottom-up* survey of the territory. A purely visual narration assembled in the everyday experience of crossing the city, from the center to the outskirts, taking unusual itineraries.

Walking through borderlines, thresholds, places of transition, empty zones and varied textures, scraps of countryside, densely edified areas, we discovered an infinite variety of incongruent features capable of generating moments of surprise and astonishment, straddling the picturesque and the sublime. We basically found ourselves crossing a multiplicity of places of transition, places between interior and exterior, *between* center and periphery, *between* city and country, places that have an inner instability.

The act of crossing the city brought us to a new image of Rome, or perhaps the same image that has fed the fantasy and creativity of many contemporary artists:[2] an image very distant from the sequence of monuments and places that forms the established imaginary of the *Eternal City*.

While the condition of instability in urban studies is often associated to a negative image, and today's global cities pursue the idea of a perfect, reassuring *stability,* Rome then is different, and if its mutable, open, unexpected instability is interpreted not as a problem but as a potential condition,[3] Rome might offer a stimulus to construct an alternative to the standardizing and generic dimensions of the contemporary city, starting with instability as a condition capable of including openness, vitality, creativity and authenticity, overturning the established equation of stability = security = well-being.

City Form – Views from the Top
Alongside the investigation *from below,* the city has been analyzed *from above,* to understand possible relations between its form – the physical condition – and the instability of its perception.

Considering Rome, like any other city, as an evolutionary organism, the research has mainly focused on the structural elements which have guided the transformation of its territory during a long formative process.[4] Convinced that not only the present form, but also any potential configuration the city can assume – what Sanford Kwinter calls the "embedded forms"[5] – is inscribed in those evolutionary mechanisms.

Redrawing the city through several maps we discovered that a few but consistent elements drove the transformation of its territory over centuries: the landscape, with its symbolic power and physical constraints – topography, water, morphology – and the radial structure of the Roman consular road, the real political form. No major planning process, nor strong external rules; Rome followed a kind of natural growing process (the speculative forces followed the same natural pattern).
The result is that of a territory substantially characterized by two closely connected phenomena: – an urban structure organized in islands, each in turn different in fab-

Labics: Maria Claudia Clemente Francesco Isidori

ric, density and typologies; – the presence of a complex, articulated constellation of voids – which as a whole represent over 70 percent of the urban territory of 129,000 hectares – ranging from small natural spaces to the large green islands of the *Ager Romanus*.[6]

This is why the actual Rome over time has always been interpreted along two form-manifestos: on one side, that of the Archipelago,[7] which is about built islands in a continuous, unbuilt natural space; on the other side, that of a great Piranesian

Paolo Canevari, Colosseao, 2000 (Marc Andreini)
Martin Parr, Roma, 2006 (Magnum/Contrasto)
Labics, Roma

Campo Marzio[8] of 2,700,000 inhabitants,[9] which is about incoherent, built islands, one next to the other. Both images are in a way similar, based on an additive logic of incoherent pieces – which is part of the DNA of the city.

But is this the only possible image? Can we find a new image for the city, which is coherent with its genealogy and its actual form? Able to incorporate the immateriality and the openness of the unstable condition but at the same time able to activate, connect, and reinforce most of the recent urban islands disconnected from the rest of the city?

An Emerging Structure for Rome – The Network of the Borders
The present form of the city of Rome probably allows for a different and more fertile interpretation than the one of *Archipelago or Campo Marzio:* the formal structure in islands, by nature, multiplies the edge condition with its true variegated set of material and immaterial features. This borderline condition can be seen as a phenomenon of "retroactive" consciousness of a strong structural presence that has not yet taken on either a clear organization or the necessary awareness within the metropolitan territory. The system of edges could become, if made explicit, a new structural pattern for the growth and development of the city, capable of connecting centers and outskirts, full and empty zones, different city portions, while being a tool to gain renewed aesthetic awareness of the cityscape.

Borderline Metropolis develops an hypothesis according to which the existing system of edges can be interpreted as an active tool for the transformation of the city. A network that is able to react, and consequently change the quality of the border in the areas where the city is weaker. In the case of Rome, for example, where a lack of density or connectivity is revealed, or where a mono-functional character of neighborhood prevails, or where the spatial qualities of the cityscape are extremely poor. The activation of the borderlines could thus become the driving force for the renewal of entire urban areas[10] and reinforce the public character of the city: Borderline Metropolis, in fact, combines in-depth analysis of the metropolitan territory with the definition of methods and tools to reactivate the borders, transforming the disconnected voids, reconnecting the inactive parts of the city, treating the territory as a whole and thus permitting a differentiated form of organization of the metropolitan territory.

Learning from Rome
Can the Borderline Metropolis be interpreted as a model for the transformation of other cities? Can Rome be seen as an antidote against the generic aspects of global cities?

The form of the city in itself can be considered as a model in its own right: a discontinuous city composed of an infinite series of different ecologies, whose perfect imbalance determines a unique urban territory rich in variety and differences.

But Borderline Metropolis goes beyond that: it advances an idea of the city and a model for its transformation at the same time. It proposes an organization that goes beyond the closed form of traditional planning and the idea of the city made of stable centers and defined city fabric. Borderline Metropolis moves towards an open, reticular, flexible conception of the city, able to respond to the needs of the territory and its inhabitants in a local and at the same time general way. The system of edges is thus a new infrastructure that can be activated and manipulated according to the needs. As a model, the network is a tool that differs from those normally used in urban planning, because it is constantly capable of updating and modifying itself based on changes in the urban fabric and knowledge regarding the complexity of processes of transformation.[11]

Finally, Borderline Metropolis does not give up on the necessity of a symbolic form behind the project of the city and, at the same time, it does not surrender to the free market approach of *laissez-faire,* or to the ideological approach of the bottom-up planning as a recipe to the progressive city gentrification. Borderline Metropolis does

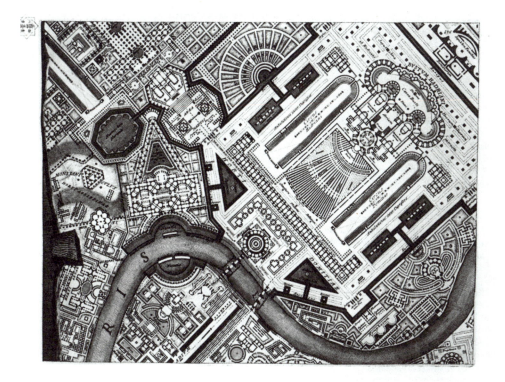

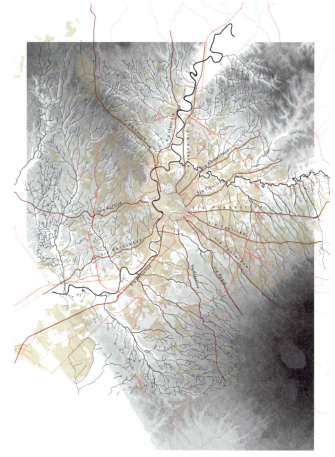

Giovanni Battista Piranesi,
Ichnographia of the Campo Marzio,
1762
Labics, Topography / Hydrography /
Roman consular system /
Contemporary structures and city

not impose an a priori form but defines the structure of the form: the idea of the network is the one of an open evolutionary form that transforms itself like an organism, and that is capable to melt values of diversity and creativity together with a structured urban system.

1   The idea of Borderline Metropolis began in 2008 when we were invited to participate in the Venice Biennale, in the exhibition *Uneternal City. Urbanism Beyond Rome,* Section of the 11th International Architecture Exhibition, directed by Aaron Betsky, 14–33

2   We are especially referring to the cinema, with artists like Federico Fellini, Pierpaolo Pasolini, and photography; for an interesting overview on the contemporary photography on Rome: Marco Delogu, Chiara Capodici, "Rome: the travelling gaze" in *Uneternal City. Urbanism Beyond Rome,* Section of the 11th International Architecture Exhibition, Marsilio, 2008.

3   In the scientific literature on complex organisms the concept of instability is fundamental, because it permits the dynamic of self-organization and changes of state. Klaus Mainzer, "Strategies for shaping complexity in nature, society and architecture" in Complexity. Design Strategy and World View, ed. Andrea Gleininger and George Vrachliotis, Basel: Birkhauser, 2008.

4   As Cassirer reminds us, the truly ideal method, for Goethe, "consists in discovering the durable in the transient, the permanent in the changeable." For Goethe, even in the most irregular phenomena it is necessary to manage to glimpse a rule that remains "fixed and inviolable." Ernst Cassirer, "Structuralism in Modern Linguistics", 1945.

5   Sanford Kwinter, "Who's afraid of formalism?", ANY Magazine 7/8 (1994).

6   Of this territory, 48 % is agricultural; 15 % is for green areas; 37 %, equal to 47,730 hectares, hosts construction.

7   This term substantially coined in the 1970s has recently come back into vogue as a possible solution to the mega-dimension of contemporary cities; the advantages of the "archipelago model" are, in fact, undoubtedly discontinuity, variation of scale and the possible construction of multiple identities; the risks are mainly the organization of the city into independent, separate enclaves, deprived of social and functional connections; the disappearing city is the scenario of the project of Oswald Mathias Ungers for Berlin, certainly the most important and significant model of an Archipelago City: The City in the City. Berlin: A Green Archipelago, ed. Florian Hertweck and Sébastien Marot, Zurich: Lars Muller, 2013 (Critical Edition, Original 1977).

8   Colin Rowe and Fred Koetter, *Collage City* (Cambridge: The MIT Press, 1983) 106–107.

9   Pier Vittorio Aureli, "Instauratio Urbis. Piranesi's Campo Marzio versus Nolli's Nuova Pianta di Roma" in Pier Vittorio Aureli, *The Possibility of an Absolute Architecture.* Cambridge: The MIT Press, 2011, 85–140.

10   During the course of the work, instability has been analyzed through four parameters;
– Connectivity: which expresses and measures the capacity of a city portion to connect with adjacent areas and with the system in general;
– Density: which expresses and measures the concentration and compactness of a city portion;
– Functionality: which expresses and measures the level of functioning of a city portion, where functioning is defined as the capacity to satisfy the different needs of the inhabitants;
– Visual quality: which expresses and measures the capacity of a city portion to possess a physical and visual identity.

11   "If there is to be a 'new urbanism' (…) it will no longer be concerned with the arrangement of more or less permanent objects but with the irrigation of territories with potential; it will no longer be obsessed with the city but with the manipulation of infrastructure for endless intensification and diversification": Rem Koolhaas, "What ever happened to Urbanism?" in *S,M,L,XL,* ed. Rem Koolhaas and Bruce Mau, New York: Moncelli Press, 1995.

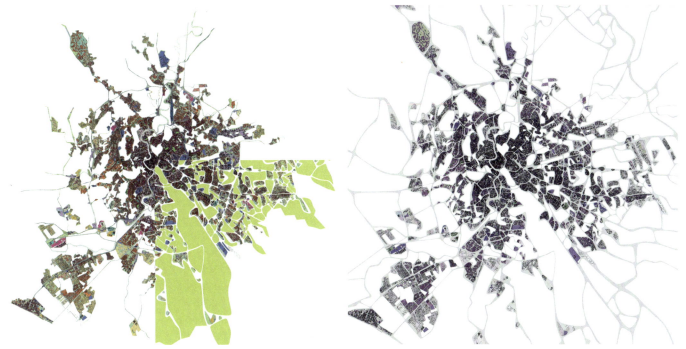

Labics, The islands and the emerging structure, Roma
Labics, The structure of borders, Roma
Labics, Model of Rome

Domestic Forms

The Architecture of the City and the Beauty of Chaos
"I am of the opinion that the contemporary Japanese city which emerged in the half-century after World War II should be recognized as the newest element of any legitimate Japanese [architectural] tradition, whose quiet beauty had persisted from ancient times down to one hundred years or so ago [...] There is no reason to deny, or nullify, this gigantic collective, which is the product of tremendous human time and energy. My view of our cities is not limited to Tokyo, for even in smaller and less affluent cities I perceive beauty but never ugliness."[1]

When I first entered Tokyo Institute of Technology I didn't expect to recognize that many students had among their books a fully translated Japanese version of *The Architecture of the City.* This fact made me consider how far the legacy of Rossi had reached and also question how the latter could be received in such diverse urban environments. At the time, most of the non-Japanese students just enrolled were focusing on gaining an overview of Kazuo Shinohara's oeuvre of residential masterpieces. While setting in the new urban environment, to catch my attention was his statement about the urban space, better known as the theory of the "Beauty of Chaos." His affirmative recognition of the chaotic form of the city offered me a sort of comforting perspective. It was able, in fact, to legitimate a kind of irrational positive reaction that emerged in me while observing the scenario of Tokyo's neighborhoods and the daily life arising from the streets, so seductive that it was easily putting into question any notion of the European city learned so far.

Through the House, Towards the City
The theory of the "Beauty of Chaos" was also very revealing to highlight a link between the individual building and the city. The houses of Kazuo Shinohara appear, in fact, with a certain degree of autonomy and abstraction, so that a connection between his spatial research and the urban space may not be predictable. Yet, the roots of Shinohara's urban theory did arise exactly through the experiences with his earliest house designs, as Shin-Ichi Okuyama points out: "And we must take seriously his youthful intuition that, in the Japanese postwar era, the only way to transform the design of private houses into an essentially architectural issue was to confront the city and its implication for society head on."[2] At the same time, we are also warned against misunderstanding that the two stand in a direct and straightforward relation to each other: "any purely linear relationship between house and city meant little to him [...] any real recovery could never spring from a single ideal logic but rather from a far more complex collective desire resulting, in turn, from a multitude of individual contexts."[3]

Decades later, another enlightening interpretation of the Japanese city develops within the framework of the individual building, offering a key to understand the possible role of the dwelling in the future of the contemporary city. *Tokyo Metabolizing,* presented by Koh Kitayama, Yoshiharu Tsukamoto and Ryue Nishizawa at the Japanese Pavilion of Venice Biennale in 2010, starting again from a lucid observation of the peculiar character of the Japanese city, reveals the potential of an initiative taken at the micro scale of the single-family house: "Unlike the urban structures one finds in Europe that were created with a series of walls, Tokyo consist of an assemblage of independent buildings (grains). In other words, constant change is an inherent part of the system. In examining the unique aspects of this unceasing change, one realizes that the city of Tokyo is an incubator for new forms of architecture and urban architectural theories [...] Tokyo has the potential to create change in the city through the quiet accumulation of urban elements rooted in daily life."[4] Through the gaze on the contemporary urban environment, the house is revealed as an active architectural form of the Japanese city.

On the other hand, the Japanese house is a well-known "object" of interest, which earned great attention internationally. The popularity and fascination for the Japanese dwelling goes back to the early modern period and extends until today.

229 Simona Ferrari

Meguro-ku
House in Uehara (Kazuo Shinohara)
House in Kyodo (Go Hasegawa)
Setagaya-ku

Instead of architects returning us careful surveys of these houses embedded in a culture of people performing completely unknown lifestyles,[5] nowadays contemporary architectural media are mainly reporting to us the latest house designs. Yet running the risk that by omitting contextual implications – as if global standards have flattened cultural differences and lifestyles to a certain extent that we feel confident to bypass them – the Japanese contemporary dwelling, detached from its history and specific environment, might appear merely as a collection of eccentric forms.

Again, only by locating the house within the framework of the city – which means to position it within the physical and social context that has produced it – we can return its significance, not only as catalyst element of the urban environment, but also as key to access, and understanding an entire culture. Since the reconstruction of the modern city, Japanese architects have committed themselves to seeking a form of architecture for life in the contemporary city through the design of the individual dwelling. In doing so, they have been re-defining spatial hierarchies, relations between the domestic and public spheres, between interior and exterior space; they have expressed their position between tradition and modernity, investigating the use of materials and construction techniques. The modern Japanese house thus assumes the value of a *collective* element of the city, carrying the legacy of the post-war Japanese society.

A Parallel City of Domestic Uniqueness
Through the individual collaboration between the architect and the client – or by the architect as client himself – the diverse combination of the abovementioned themes has resulted in a rich architectural production of distinct dwellings, where perhaps the sole aspect truly shared among all of these houses is exactly their character of *uniqueness.* Certain houses came to represent some of the most known masterpieces of Japanese modern architecture. Since Japan is no longer the far and unreachable country it used to be, today many architects undergo an architectural pilgrimage to these houses. Yet, spread along a territory divided by 1.8 million owners[6] these domestic architectures are nothing more than a rarefied constellation of small fragments that sums up to the vast chaotic landscape of the city. The encounter of one of these dwellings is mostly likely to be an accidental and fortuitous discovery of the urban *flâneur* who wonders around Tokyo's neighborhoods. Far from constituting an accumulation that could be examined as a *dwelling* area or manifesting any recognizable typology, the Japanese house designed by the architect is a *unicum* distinguished by its form and unique character within the urban environment.[7] Only in our minds do all these houses form a parallel city of housing uniqueness.

Punctual and exceptional element of the city, the House, with its active and collective character, may be understood as a kind of scattered *urban artifact*[8] hidden in the urban fabric of the Japanese city.

Epilogue
Both Shinohara and Rossi define, respectively, the House and the Urban Artifact as *works of art.* "The House is a Work of Art" is among Shinohara's most recognised statements, which, together with the "Beauty of Chaos," have conveyed his criticism toward the architectural scene of his time.[9] For Rossi, the status of "The Urban Artifact as a Work of Art" is bound to the collective and unique character of urban artifacts as well as a fundamental theme raised by several theorists.[10] Nevertheless, both definitions are embedded with their own specific reasoning; this fortuitous analogy provides the hint to recognize that both European and Japanese understandings of the city may coexist with their resonances and diversities to grasp aspects of our living environment.

Small House (Kazuyo Sejima)
Shinjuku-ku
House & atelier Bow-Wow (Atelier Bow-Wow)
Shinjuku-ku

1   K. Shinohara, "Toward a Super-Big Numbers Set City and a Small House Beyond," in: *2G* N.58/59, Kazuo Shinohara Houses, Barcelona, 2011 p. 279
2   S. Okuyama, "Words and Spaces: How Kazuo Shinohara's Thought spans between Residential and Urban Theory," in: *2G* N.58/59, Kazuo Shinohara Houses, Barcelona, 2011.
3   See previous reference.
4   K. Kitayama, Y. Tsukamoto, R. Nishizawa, *Tokyo Metabolizing*, TOTO Shuppan, Tokyo, 2010; p. 11
5   B. Taut, *Houses and People of Japan*.
6   See reference 4 p. 129
7, 8   With reference to the definition of urban artifacts, primary elements and dwelling areas, in: A. Rossi, *The Architecture of the City*, the MIT Press, New York, 1982.
9   See reference 2.
10   A. Rossi, "The Urban Artifact as a Work of Art" in: A. Rossi, *The Architecture of the City*, the MIT Press, New York, 1982.

Shinjuku-ku

Invisible Infrastructures and Their Forms

We shall not begin with the description of a Parallel City, either desired or dystopian, for to even attempt this, one first needs to question the given facts and recognize the running simulcasts that form each reality. Exactly as in Calvino's Berenic,[1] deducing an image of an urban complex requires knowledge about the hidden, underlying mechanisms and networks that power the "here and now."

Understood in a broad sense, such mechanisms are properly infrastructural; conduits accommodating flows of commodities and information in physical space. There is no need to dig the earth to reach for them, though; conventional infrastructures like highways, terminals and ports, as well as unconventional ones like malls, mass-generated suburbs and free trade zones are well expanding on the surface, although they consistently try to hide themselves from plain sight. The question of Form in infrastructural projects evolves into a major issue, as it is this which is nowadays able to control both the image and the organization of territories. Returning to the layers of reality, with infrastructure in mind, we intend to go one step deeper, in order to comprehend the background activities and narratives that shape them. Deciphering the back-end algorithms that run their systems essentially means to understand the form of their form.

Infrastructures and their gestalt are considered both by the general public and the technical experts a not-to-be-challenged issue. Distancing themselves from the idea of the "public work," their "whys" and "hows," their scope and their design, are obvious results of the dominant techno-managerial school of thought, favoring the tried-and-true paradigm of efficiency and growth. For infrastructures were built upon the beliefs shaped throughout modernity, namely functionality, economic efficiency and social homogeneity, and consolidated throughout supermodernity with globalization and the rise of what Easterling calls Extrastatecraft.[2] What's important here is that the mindset described applies not only to infrastructures' actual organization and structure, but also to their most latent narratives.

Having said the above, the dogma of a frictionless running system outlines two distinct possibilities for the infrastructural spatial products: On the one hand, efficiency may be understood in a literal way, resulting in properly rationalized constructions where function is an end in itself. On the other hand, efficiency may be used merely as a justifying motive, producing much more of a theatrical setting than a serving mechanism. We will call these two distinguishable categories infrastructures of *Superfunction* and *Superform,* respectively.

The rationale of the first category is perceived in the light of scientific and technological cultures introduced in architectural thought throughout modernity. The founding declaration of the CIAM, signed in La Sarraz in 1928, communicated the agony for rationalization and universalization in the field, with its first points referring not to architecture itself but to the "General Economic System."[3] Standardization and technical specifications mark the rise of the engineers, whom Le Corbusier himself was praising. Infrastructure space constitutes the most appropriate field for this system of thought to be practiced, therefore transforming it to mere technical elements of the urban whole. In infrastructures of Superfunction, the form of their form is actually more like a rigid diagram: the same diagram that defines functions and specifications, indicated by a specialized engineer or a developer-manager. Let's bring to mind images of rectangular warehouses like that of e-shops, mall-like big box stores like the IKEAs, commercial ports as well as enclaves of special economic zones like industrial and logistic parks. In spaces like these, shape and image are irrelevant; a working diagram and a generic lot are just enough. The actual surroundings play no role, that way annihilating another component which defines form. Relations to the place, the neighboring structures or the environment are ignored as potential distractions. These infrastructures are placed not just as if on a *tabula rasa,* but even more, separating themselves from the context with fences, guarded gates and buffer

George Papam Papamattheakis
George Foufas

Invisible infrastructures. Camouflaged antenna in the form of a palm tree.

zones. Stripped of any identity or meaning, these heavy functional and closed systems, although coherent in themselves, are essentially machines-in-a-box scattered around. All in all, "form follows function," in its extreme, means we can do without form anyway.

On the other hand, infrastructures of Superform seem to emanate from the postmodern over-investment in meaning. Disregarding anything modern, the obsession against strict functionality is combined with the love for the spectacle that characterizes our times. Given that infrastructures have the inherent potential to operate at the level of fantasy and desire and at that of collective subconscious,[4] these dynamics are being exploited to achieve a different kind of function, namely that of symbolism. Productive efficiency and growth are put aside, making room for a communication mechanism of structured narratives. Still, being accountable to the wider dogma of efficiency, and in order to justify themselves, these irrational or distorted infrastructures invoke stories of progress and modernization as perceptual tricks. In Superform infrastructures, the form of their form is more like an image; a glossy advertisement of what is not there. Typical examples of this condition are highways and artificial landscapes in Dubais around the world, as well as squares and factories constructed by authoritarian regimes promoting their industrial "prevalence." Unduly massive, they were not designed to address a social need or achieve a production goal, rather to broadcast a message of economic or political progress. Actual function is disassociated from form, and the remaining structures are embellished and finally sold back either as monument or spectacle. Context as part of the form is defied again, unless it can be instrumentally used as appealing feature of the product on sale. These infrastructures are further stripped off from their fundamental signification as shared means to common ends, in order to propagate power and forward images of economic dominance. The aestheticised infrastructures finally have no form, but rather shape.

Both these practices have a common end: They tend to disregard the spatial impact of an object, usually immense in scale, and the collateral repercussions it produces on the organization of the nearby land and its production systems, services and social structures. Yet, we argue that the political power of infrastructural space lies exactly at the decisions that form the object itself and the way it interacts with its surroundings. Especially in the case of infrastructure, these choices are not static, predefined or steadfast. In its operational life cycle, an infrastructural project can re-evaluate its goals and practices and therefore radically transform an urban complex by giving priority to certain activities over others.[5] This responsibility should not be overlooked in the name of a ubiquitous and self-evident system or a provocative, flashy image.

In the condition of a Parallel City, each infrastructural project could be seen as a place for experimentation, acknowledging the possibility of unpredicted outcomes and opposing the dogma of an over-designed, fully-determinate plan produced by a closed set of rules, standards and indexes. The obvious need for efficiency can't be disregarded; yet it is political discourse which should describe the type and parameters of the efficiency each infrastructure aims to. Without a predefined answer, in a Rancierian context, we argue that public spaces, like infrastructures, have to be constantly questioned and therefore regenerated, with the given identities, labels and statuses each time in dispute.

1   Italo Calvino, *Invisible Cities,* New York: Harcourt Brace Jovanovich, 1974.
2   Keller Easterling, *Extrastatecraft: The Power of Infrastructure Space,* London: Verso, 2014.
3   Ulrich Conrads, "CIAM: La Sarraz Declaration," in *Programs and Manifestoes on 20th-century Architecture,* 109–13, Cambridge, MA: MIT Press, 1971.
4   See Brian Larkin, "The Politics and Poetics of Infrastructure," *Annual Review of Anthropology* 42, no. 1 (2013): 327–43 as well as Sam Jacob, "Ceci N'Est Pas Une Pipe: Infrastructure as Architectural Subconcious," Strange Harvest (blog). http:// strangeharvest.com/ ceci-nest-pas-une-pipe-infrastructure-as-architectural-subconcious.
5   See Ashley Carse, "Nature as Infrastructure: Making and Managing the Panama Canal Watershed," *Social Studies of Science* 42, no. 4 (2012): 557. "When a landform is assigned value in relation to one cultural system of production (transportation) rather than another (agriculture), different environmental services become relevant and the landscape is reorganized to prioritize the delivery of those services and support that system. This calls us to examine the ethics of making natural infrastructure and to ask how systems […] might be managed in a manner that is more just
and equitable […]"

Superfunction. Possible to be found anywhere in the world: indentical warehouses as a result of a spatial formula.
Superform. Twenty-lane highway in Myanmar's administrative capital, a city of less than a million people.

Time Catalyst Forms

This essay will explore the idea of time in the making of cities, landscapes or architectures.

I. A possible strategy to do so would be finding existing structures, "as found" spaces, or fragmentary traces, in order to reinhabit and transform them. This way, anticipatory forms would be identified and transformed by being dwelled in in a different way, and so extending or stretching their lifetime.

II. However, rather than simply identifying such forms, the intent of this essay is to explore the possibility of making formal propositions (both new and as enhancements of existing fragments) that may allow for former inhabitation as well as later transformation. In other words, using these instigator forms as design tools and as catalysts that anticipate and enable a future territory, city or building change over the course of time. Forms charged with these foreseeing qualities might be called "time catalyst forms."
– Time catalyst forms might be spaces (voids in-between) or physical bodies (topographies, buildings, elements). They might be barely recognizable, immaterial or invisible. Otherwise, they could be signs and artefacts clearly inscribed in the human sight. They might also be collective memories, urban legislation or social dynamics.
– Time catalyst forms anticipate program; however, they must foresee multiple ways of inhabitation.
– If city or architectural elements might be envisaged either as permanent or temporary, time catalyst forms would be the former, lasting throughout indefinite time and enabling temporary dwelling or any trace of existence to arise. These permanent forms would usually be erected in heavy stone or rough concrete, opposite to their inhabitation, often assembled in timber boards or soft textiles. However, in alternative instances, it could be the other way around, with pivoting panels, bouncy castles, small furniture or even communal stories and festivities making possible the transformation of temporary streets, squares and buildings.
– Time catalyst forms should be conceived at varying scales (spatially and temporarily). At a larger scale, certain time catalyst forms might be considered provisional occupation and at a smaller scale, remnants of inhabitation might become time catalyst forms. Sheltered valleys might be seen as rooms and inland lakes as courtyards from which city inhabitation begins. Delicate topographies, fragmentary dry stone terraces, forgotten paths or canals along large farming fields, might indicate future forms of expansion. Agricultural or urban plots, their open-ended structure expanding through horizontal terrain, might be seen as bookshelves to be designed foreseeing the inhabitation of a rich variety of biographies and belongings; allowing for diverse and collective types of constructions, buildings or plantations, one next to the other; making possible a common making of territories and cities. Permanent building interiors, between distant concrete slabs or masonry walls, might be seen as large public spaces, permitting smaller partitions or furniture – such as little house or forests – to occupy the space temporarily. Small cabinets or benches, somehow designed as buildings, might be seen as permanent landmarks to discover and inhabit momentarily. An approaching hand may be seen as a landscape to be explored.
– Time catalyst forms should have an interesting physical relationship with their future inhabitants, so as to be recognizable, meaningful and anticipate forthcoming collective civic life. Qualities to define such "interesting forms" might be diverse. Primarily, interesting forms should find a sense of size, a sense of weight, a sense of touch; they should find specific and interesting dimensions, shapes and material qualities that our sight might (somehow primitively) understand in order to become sensitive envelopes foreseeing the rhythm of life; anticipating the tone of our conversations, the speed of our walk or the silence of our contemplation. Interesting forms should also find a sense of sequence, a feeling of the contrast experienced between one form and the next; stressing binary oppositions to make themselves

clearly readable or conversely, drawing attention to subtle alterations on pale colors to capture a grasp of change in calmness. Likewise, interesting forms might inscribe charged qualities of our cultural constructs, collective memories, ethical beliefs, political principles or even the beauty of transcendental uselessness or banal pleasure; sometimes in the form of sign or symbol and other times as fragmentary gestures unveiled behind our misted glasses.

222 In-Formed Lisbon

The contemporary metropolis erases the traditional conception of context altogether its basis relying on its continuous management of content, with a dialogue among its actors and the *interchangeability* of their forms. By admitting the continuous process of *un-contextualization* of our metropolises, we are assuming a way of urbanism that does not rely on the shape of an urban fabric anymore, but instead on the in-formation of its networks, of its infrastructures and scenarios. The tension within this contradictory paradigm is what rules its machinery.

In-formed Lisbon assumes these contradictions as an inherent condition of the contemporary city. Hence, *In-formed Lisbon* compiles a series of "sampled urbanisms" which, imported from other contexts and using the city as a motherboard, are plugged in to Lisbon, generating a catalogue of *faked realities.*

They point out four urban situations that do not depend on the city's shape but on its *performability.* A political artefact acting as architecture. A process of transforming an architectural piece into an economical machine. A natural element converted into a human infrastructure. A peer-to-peer revolution.

They correspond to four processes of generating urbanism that are *self-textualized,* being contexts themselves.

Within *In-formed Lisbon,* it is the content that becomes the context.

Lisbon Wall – "A Political Artefact as Architecture"
The *Lisbon Wall* (Portuguese: O Muro de Lisboa) was a barrier that divided Lisbon from 1961 to 1989. Constructed by the *Portuguese Democratic Republic* (PDR, South Portugal), starting on 13 August 1961, *the Wall* completely cut off (by land) *North Lisbon* from surrounding *South Portugal* and from *South Lisbon* until government officials opened it in November 1989. Its demolition officially began on 13 June 1990 and was completed in 1992. The barrier included guard towers placed along large concrete walls, which circumscribed a wide area (later known as the "death strip") that contained anti-vehicle trenches, *fakir beds* and other defences. The Southern Bloc claimed that *the Wall* was erected to protect its population from fascist elements conspiring to prevent the "will of the people" in building a socialist state in South Portugal. In practice, *the Wall* served to prevent the massive emigration and defection that had marked *South Portugal* and the communist *Southern Bloc* during the post-World War II period. [...]

The fall of the *Lisbon Wall* paved the way for *Portuguese reunification,* which was formally concluded on 3 October 1990.

Lisboa Effect – "Iconism as Urbanism"
The *Lisboa Effect* is a portmanteau used to describe the urban process of introducing a singular piece of architecture into a city's urban fabric with the aim of transforming its contexts by means of a political and economical shift. By the usage of an icon, a process of urbanization of an area is generated.

Such an urban mechanism has ruled the processes of urban development of the cities' centers around the globe during the 90s. Cities were worried about "reinventing themselves," giving precedence to the value given by culture. Municipalities and non-profit organizations hoped the use of a *Starchitect* would drive traffic and tourist income to their new facilities. With the popular and critical success of the *Guggenheim Museum in Lisboa,* by Frank Gehry, in which a rundown area of a city in economic decline brought in huge financial growth and prestige, the media started to talk about the so-called "Lisboa Effect." A star architect designing a blue-chip, prestige building was thought to make all the difference in producing a landmark for the city.

Developers around the world have used this mechanism as a prototype for replication in the quest of convincing reluctant municipalities to approve large developments, obtaining financing or increasing the value of their buildings.

Pedro Pitarch

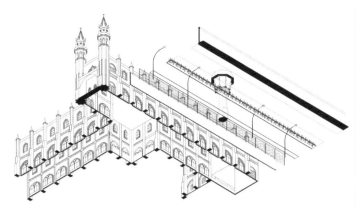

Axonometric View of a section of the Lisbon Wall next to Mosteiro dos Jerónimos
Google Maps Screenshot of the surroundings of Guggenheim Lisbon at Praça do Comercio
Official Site Plan of the Tagus Port City as defined by NATO
Protest movement at Parque Eduardo VII, while marching towards Praça Marquês de Pombal

Tagus Port City – "The River as Infrastructure"
The *Tagus Port City* (Portuguese: *Cidade portuária de Tejo*) is the largest port in Europe, located in the city of Lisbon. From 1962 until 2004 it was the world's busiest port, now overtaken first by Singapore and then Shanghai. In 2011, Lisbon was the world's eleventh-largest container port in terms of twenty-foot equivalent units (TEU) handled. Covering 105 square kilometers (41 sq mi), the port of Lisbon now stretches over a distance of 40 kilometers (25 mi).

Much of the container loading and stacking in the port is handled by autonomous robotic cranes and computer-controlled chariots. The *Lisbon Droid Inc.* pioneered the development of terminal automation. At the *Tagus Terminal,* the chariots – or *auto-*

mated guided vehicles (AGV) – are unmanned, and each carries one container. The chariots navigate their own way around the terminal with the help of a magnetic grid built into the terminal tarmac. Once a container is loaded onto an AGV, it is identified by infrared "eyes" and delivered to its designated place within the terminal. This terminal is also named *the ghost terminal.*

The port is operated by Tagus City, originally a municipal body of the city of Lisbon, but since January 1, 2004, a self-governed corporation declared an *autonomous microstate* regulated by NATO.

Occupy Marquês de Pombal – "A Peer to Peer Revolution"
Occupy Marquês de Pombal (OMP) is the name given to a protest movement that began on September 17, 2011, in Parque Eduardo VII, located in Lisboa's Marquês de Pombal financial district, receiving global attention and spawning the *Occupy* movement against social and economic inequality worldwide. It was inspired by anti-austerity protests in Spain coming from the *15-M Movement.*

The Portuguese, anti-consumerist, pro-environment group/magazine *Publi-Cidade* initiated the call for a protest.

The main issues raised by *Occupy Marquês de Pombal* were social and economic inequality, greed, corruption and the perceived undue influence of corporations on government – particularly from the financial services sector. The OMP slogan, "We are the 99 %," refers to income inequality and wealth distribution between the wealthiest 1 % and the rest of the population. To achieve their goals, protesters acted on consensus-based decisions made in general assemblies, which emphasized direct action over petitioning authorities for redress.

The protesters were forced out of Parque Eduardo VII on November 15, 2011. Protesters turned their focus to occupying banks, corporate headquarters, board meetings, foreclosed homes and college and university campuses.

Bureau A (15) (128)
BUREAU A (2012–2017) was the association of Leopold Banchini and Daniel Zamarbide, architects by training. BUREAU A was a multidisciplinary platform aiming to blur the boundaries of research and project-making on architecture-related subjects, whatever their nature and status.

Åbäke (34)
Åbäke is a transdisciplinary graphic design collective, founded in 2000 by Patrick Lacey (UK), Benjamin Reichen (FR), Kajsa Ståhl (SE) and Maki Suzuki (FR) in London, England, after they met at the Royal College of Art. Members of Åbäke co-founded *Sexymachinery* (Magazine, 2000–2008), Kitsuné (Record label, 2002), Dent-De-Leone (publishing house, 2009) and *Drawing Room Confession* (Journal 2011). They have taught at RCA (2004–2010), Central St Martins (2005–2015), IUAV (2009), HEAD (2012–ongoing), Isia Urbino (2013), Camberwell (2015), Chelsea (2015) and Yale (2015)

Noura Al-Sayeh (43)
Noura Al-Sayeh is an architect currently working at the Bahrain Authority for Culture and Antiquities (BACA) as Head of Architectural Affairs, where she is responsible for overseeing the planning and implementation of cultural institutions and museums as well as the creation of an active agenda of exhibitions and academic exchange initiatives. Previously, she worked as an architect in New York, Jerusalem and Amsterdam. She was the co-curator of *Reclaim,* Bahrain's first participation at the 12th Venice Architecture Biennale in 2010, which was awarded the Golden Lion for best national participation, and the curator of *Background,* Bahrain's second participation at the Venice Architecture Biennale in 2012. She was the commissioner of *Fundamentalists and Other Arab Modernisms,* Bahrain's third participation at the Venice Architecture Biennale, as well as the Deputy Commissioner General for *Archeaologies of Green,* Bahrain's National Pavilion at the Expo Milan 2015, which was awarded a silver medal for best architecture and landscape. Alongside her work for the BACA, she works as an independent architect.

Annette Amberg (112)
Annette Amberg is an artist living in Zurich. Solo exhibitions include *Mother (Working Title),* Le Foyer, Zurich (2015); *Una questione privata,* Istituto Svizzero di Roma (2014); *Everything But Arms,* Kunsthaus Glarus (2012). Amberg worked as assistant curator at Kunsthalle Basel from 2007 until 2011. She runs her own curatorial projects with different collaborators, among them Amberg & Marti (2005–07) and Q (ongoing).

Pier Vittorio Aureli (144)
Pier Vittorio Aureli studied at the Istituto Universitario di Architettura di Venezia and later at the Berlage Institute in Rottedam. Aureli currently teaches at the AA School of Architecture in London and is visiting professor at Yale University. He is the author of many essays and several books, including *The Project of Autonomy* (2008) and *The Possibility of an Absolute Architecture* (2011).

Babau Bureau (198)
BABAU BUREAU is an architectural and landscape office founded in 2012 by Stefano Tornieri and Massimo Triches in Venice. BABAU BUREAU's current research focuses on the reuse and transformation of buildings and open spaces as a contemporary requirement and as a sustainable development strategy. Beside their professional careers, the members of the office conducte an active research in the academic field, working in the "Architecture and Archaeologies of the Production Landscapes" research unit of the IUAV University of Venice.

Stefano Tornieri, b. 1985, architect. Master's degree in architecture at IUAV of Venice and ETSAB of Barcelona. Currently a post-doctoral researcher at IUAV of Venice. He worked in Venice, Italy; Hierapolis, Turkey and Lisbon, Portugal.

Massimo Triches, b. 1984, architect. Master degree in landscape architecture at IUAV of Venice and ETSAB of Barcelona. He worked in Venice, Italy; Valencia, Spain; Rosario, Argentina and Manchester, England. PhD in architectural composition.

Chiara Davino, b. 1994, Bachelor's degree in architecture at IUAV of Venice. She collaborated with Renato Rizzi as assistant professor and with Babau Bureau in competitions and theoretical research.

Pau Bajet (220)
Pau Bajet (architect ARB COAC) studied architecture at the Barcelona School of Architecture (ETSAB), where he graduated with honors, tutored by Eduard Bru. He worked as an architect in London for David Chipperfield Architects before establishing Bajet Girame Architects in 2015. He was recently awarded La Caixa Fellowship for Postgraduate Studies to complete a PhD "by design," supervised by Florian Beigel and Philip Christou, at the Architectural Research Unit of the Sir John Cass Faculty of Art, Architecture and Design (LondonMet). He is currently teaching at ARU's studio at the Cass, had previously been Visiting Lecturer at the Birmingham City University and Teaching Assistant for four years at the Barcelona School of Architecture. His work has been awarded in several competitions, published and exhibited in Spain, Germany, the UK, Austria, Italy and Greece.

162 Baukuh
baukuh produces architecture.
Designs are independent of personal taste. No member of baukuh is ever individually responsible for any single project, each of which is the product of the office as a whole. Working without a hierarchical structure or a stylistic dogma, baukuh produces architecture out of a rational and explicit design process. This process is based on a critical understanding of the architecture of the past. The knowledge encoded in the architecture of the past is public, and starting from this public knowledge, any architectural problem can be solved.

102 Adrià Carbonell
Adrià Carbonell is an architect and educator based in Stockholm. He is Visiting Professor at KU Leuven, and has held teaching positions at Umeå School of Architecture and at the American University of Sharjah.

26 Amateur Cities
Amateur Cities is an online publishing platform on alternative ways of citymaking presented critically. It aims to connect city thinkers to city makers.
Amateur Cities publishes articles that collect, analyze and clarify contemporary urban and technological development, which can be interesting for discovering cities anew – not as masters, but as amateurs. It provides a platform for a dialogue on urban collective intelligence by presenting side-by-side theoretical and practical voices. It stimulates cross-sector exchange by engaging experts from architecture, urbanism, art, science, information technology, media, sociology and philosophy.
The platform was set up and developed by Cristina Ampatzidou and Ania Molenda, with generous support from Creative Industries Fund NL.

30 Titi Balali
Titi Balali, librarian, works in Oxford.

196 Patricia Barbas
Patricia Barbas (b. Luanda, 1971) Diploma in Architecture from FAUTL, Lisbon. Collaborated with Aires Mateus, Gonçalo Byrne, and João Pedro Falcão de Campos. Guest Professor at Carleton University, Ottawa and EPFL Lausanne.

92 Shumon Basar
Shumon Basar is co-author of *The Age of Earthquakes: A Guide to the Extreme Present* with Douglas Coupland and Hans Ulrich Obrist. He is Commissioner of the Global Art Forum, Dubai; Editor-at-Large of *Tank* magazine and Contributing Editor at *Bidoun* magazine; Director of the Format program at the AA School, London; and a member of Fondazione Prada's "Thought Council."

136 Laura Bonell + Daniel López-Dòriga
Laura Bonell and Daniel López-Dòriga (b. Barcelona, 1987) both studied architecture in ETSAB. They each spent one year studying abroad, at the Accademia di Architettura di Mendrisio and the Technische Universität München respectively. They started their office together, Bonell+Dòriga, in 2014, where they work on projects at various scales: from small private commissions to public competitions. Among other places, their work has been published in the famed *Casabella* magazine, as part of their 85th anniversary issue focused on young architects.

43 Matilde Cassani
Born in 1980, Matilde Cassani studied Architecture in Milano and Lisbon, then Architecture and Urban culture at the CCCB (Centro de Cultura Contemporània de Barcelona) in Barcelona, Spain. After her graduation, Cassani worked as a consultant for GTZ (German association for technical cooperation) in Sri Lanka, where she started developing a research project on the post-tsunami reconstruction. She currently teaches at Politecnico di Milano and at Domus Academy. Her practice reflects the spatial implications of cultural pluralism in the contemporary Western urban context. Matilde Cassani often moves on the border between architecture, installation and performance. She has been a resident fellow at Akademie Schloss Solitude in Stuttgart and at the Headlands Center for the Arts in San Francisco. Storefront for Art and Architecture in New York hosted her exhibition *Sacred Spaces in Profane Buildings* in September 2011. She also designed the National Pavilion of The Kingdom of Bahrain at the 13th Venice Architecture Biennale in 2012, and she was part of the XIV Venice Architecture Biennale (Monditalia) with the piece *Countryside worship. A celebration day,* recently acquired by the Victoria and Albert Museum in London. She has taken part in many international conferences and lectured in various international Universities such as Columbia University in New York and Ecole Speciale d' Architecture in Paris.

194 Ciriacidis Lehnerer Architekten
Ciriacidis Lehnerer Architekten is a Zurich-based architectural practice led by Savvas Ciriacidis and Alex Lehnerer. The office tries to understand architecture as cultural practice. Further critical and academic discourse is resonating with the work through teaching and research activities – with Alex's position as assistant professor at ETH Zürich and Savvas's teaching at the Hochschule Luzern. Among other things, both have been the commissioners of the German pavilion at the 14th International Architecture Biennale in Venice in 2014.

64 José Pedro Cortes
José Pedro Cortes (b. Porto, Portugal, 1976) studied at Kent Institute of Art and Design (Master of Arts in Photography) in the UK. He has been exhibiting regularly during the last ten years and has published four books. He is also the founder and co-editor of Pierre von Kleist editions, a photobook publisher based in Lisbon.

76 Irina Davidovici
Irina Davidovici is postdoctoral researcher at ETH Zurich. Born in Bucharest, she qualified as an architect in London and worked with Caruso St John and Herzog & de Meuron between 1998–2002. She completed her doctorate at the University of Cambridge in 2008 and until 2012, taught history and theory of architecture at Kingston University. Her research bridges the practice, teaching, and critical interpretation of architecture, and has been published in numerous books and journals.

100 Alexandre Delmar
Alexandre Delmar (b. 1982, Porto) is an artist. He holds a Bachelor's degree in Photography from the Higher Artistic School of Porto, and a Diploma in Audiovisual Communication Techniques from the School of Music and Performing Arts of the Polytechnic Institute of Porto

38 Dieter Dietz
Educated at the Swiss Federal Institute of Technology, Zurich (Arch. Degree 1991), Dieter Dietz also studied at the Cooper Union in New York with Diller/Scofidio, Micheal Webb and Jean Scully. Since 2006, he is Associate Professor for Architectural Design at EPFL, director of the ALICE laboratory in the ENAC faculty. He collaborates with the ALICE team on research projects on diverse scales with labs and professionals inside and outside EPFL.

24 Andrea Alberto Dutto
Andrea Alberto Dutto graduated in 2010 with a dual degree at Polytechnic University of Turin and the ENSA Marseille. Since 2013 he is a PhD candidate in Architecture at Polytechnic University of Turin and since 2015, he has been developing his PhD thesis within a co-tutelle program between Turin and RWTH Aachen University where he is collaborating at "Tool-Culture."

The Junior Professorship "Tool-Culture" considers its research fields as tightly connected to its teaching activities and focusses on the instruments and methods of architectural designing. We investigate the impact of specific methodical approaches on the results of design processes, the interdependencies between a changing professional profile and the selection of design tools, and the potential of knowledge transfer between architecture and other disciplinary or scientific fields. In our didactical activities, we develop experimental setups and methods to convey productive design thinking and a general reflexivity to student.

43 Victoria Easton
Victoria Easton studied architecture at the EPF Lausanne and at the ETH Zurich, where she graduated in 2005. Since then, she works for Christ & Gantenbein, participating in many building projects as well as being nominated as a Research Associate in 2012. She has taught and lectured at the EPF Lausanne, ETH Zurich, Berlage Institute, TU Delft, IIT, Milan Politecnico and Harvard GSD. Throughout her professional and academic activity, she has been involved with research, edition and curating, elaborating on the interaction between the city and its architecture. She is a regular contributor to San Rocco magazine and editor of *Christ & Gantenbein: Around the Corner* (2012), *Typology: Hong Kong, Rome, New York, Buenos Aires* (2012) and *Typology: Paris, Delhi, São Paulo, Athens* (2015). In 2016, she curated the exhibition *The Books of* the Architecture of the City at the Istituto Svizzero Milano which focused on Aldo Rossi's seminal book. She has been a member of the Swiss Federal Art Commission since 2017.

166 Edelaar Mosayebi Inderbitzin (EMI) Architekten
Ron Edelaar, Elli Mosayebi, and Christian Inderbitzin founded their architectural firm in Zurich in 2005. The firm's broad scope of work encompasses building projects from design to construction to urban planning, along with exhibitions and publications. Housing represents a main focus of their research, teaching and practice. Since 2011, major projects have been realized through routine collaboration with Baumberger & Stegmeier Architekten. Elli Mosayebi has been Professor for Design and Housing at TU Darmstadt since 2012. Christian Inderbitzin taught at the ETH in Lausanne (EPFL) in 2015/2016. Ron Edelaar, Elli Mosayebi, and Christian Inderbitzin were enrolled as members of the Federation of Swiss Architects in 2014.

56 Mariabruna Fabrizi + Fosco Lucarelli
Mariabruna Fabrizi (*1982) and Fosco Lucarelli (*1981) are architects from Italy. They are currently based in Paris where they have founded the architectural practice Microcities and conduct independent architectural research through their website SOCKS. They work as assistant teachers at the Éav&t, in Marnes La Vallé, Paris and at EPFL, Lausanne. They are the content curators of *The Form of Form* exhibition in the 2016 Lisbon Triennale.

32 Grégoire Farquet
Coming from the Valais, Grégoire has studied at EPF Lausanne and ETH Zürich, where he graduated with

Prof. Peter Märkli's diploma class. During his study time he worked on several building transformations in rural areas of the Valais. He founded Farquet Architectes Sàrl in 2015 and regularly writes critiques for Hochparterre competitions.

210 Simona Ferrari

Simona Ferrari (1988) graduated in architecture at Politecnico di Milano. She continued her studies at the Technische Universität Wien and then at Tokyo Institute of Technology as Monbukagakusho Fellow, where she received her Master's degree, while training in several Tokyo-based architectural practices. Since 2014, she has been working with Atelier Bow-Wow on several international projects, exhibition designs and installations. Her photographic work develops in parallel to the architectural practice.

70 Ganko

Ganko produces architecture. Ganko was established in 2011 by Guido Tesio (1984) and Nicola Munaretto (1984) following previous experiences with Baukuh (Milan) and OFFICE kgdvs (Brussels). After three years spent between Milan and Beijing, in 2014 Ganko has relocated to Switzerland, where it currently lives and practices between Lausanne and Basel. Since 2012 Ganko has taken part in several projects and texts for many publications and exhibitions. In 2013, Ganko was invited to contribute to the book *Pure Hardcore Icons: A Manifesto for Pure Form in Architecture* edited by WAI Think Tank for Artifice Books, London. Since 2014, Ganko is guest editor for the catalogues of the Beijing-based art gallery Intelligentsia. Recent works by Ganko have been featured in *Domusweb, StudioMagazine* and *San-Rocco*.

134 Cloé Gattigo

Cloé Gattigo was born in 1984 and grew up in Haïti. She graduated with a Master of Arts in Architecture at the Accademia di architettura di Mendrisio in 2007. She worked as an architect for Christ & Gantenbein and as a research assistant at the Christ & Gantenbein Design studio at the ETH Zurich.

32 **182** Eric Leo Gösswald

Before graduating at Universität der Künste in his hometown Berlin, Eric has been a guest student at Studio Krucker Bates (TU München), Prof. Peter Märkli (ETH Zürich) and the painting class of Thomas Zipp (UdK Berlin). He also worked at Modersohn & Freiesleben Architekten in Berlin and Lütjens Padmanabhan Architects in Zürich.

104 Stefano Graziani

Stefano Graziani, photographer. Teaches at the Photography Master at IUAV in Venice and at Naba in Milano, collaborates with different architects: Office KGDVS, Baukuh, Federico Zanfi, 51N4E, Christ & Gantenbein, Piovene/Fabi. Founder with other colleagues of *San Rocco* Magazine and *Genda.* His work has been widely published and exhibited.

126 Owen Hatherley

Owen Hatherley was born in Southampton, England in 1981. He received a PhD in 2011 from Birkbeck College, London, for a thesis on Constructivism and Americanism, which was published in 2016 as *The Chaplin Machine* (Pluto Press). He writes regularly for *Architects Journal, Architectural Review, Dezeen, the Guardian, the London Review of Books* and *New Humanist,* and is the author of several books.

178 Anne Holtrop

Anne Holtrop (1977) graduated in 2005 from the Academie van Bouwkunst in Amsterdam with a cum laude degree in architecture, and in 2009 started his own studio. Today his office is based in Muharraq (Bahrain) and Amsterdam (The Netherlands). His work ranges from models to temporary spaces and buildings. In 2015, his first two major buildings, Museum Fort Vechten and the National Pavilion of the Kingdom of Bahrain, were completed. Both projects won several international awards. His work has been widely published in the international press and this year Walther Koenig published the 2G monograph #73 is published by Walther Koenig on his work. He is currently guest professor at the Accademia di Architettura in Mendrisio, Switzerland. For his practice, he has been awarded several grants from the Mondrian Fund, as well as receiving the Charlotte Kohler Prize for Architecture from the Prince Bernhard Culture Fund in 2007 and the Iakov Chernikhov Award 2014.

32 Anna Katharina Hüveler

Beginning her studies at RWTH Aachen, then continuing at ETH Zürich at studio Prof. Hans Kollhoff and later graduating in the diploma class of Prof. Peter Märkli, Anna has worked for Max Dudler (study for the university centre Zürich and transformation of Sihlpost Building Zürich) and later joined the office of Joseph Smolenicky (transformation of the city theatre Bern and several competitions for educational buildings).

36 Sam Jacob

Sam Jacob is principal of Sam Jacob Studio for architecture and design, a practice whose work spans scales and disciplines from urban design through architecture, design, art and curatorial projects. He has worked internationally on award-winning projects and has exhibited at major museums such as the V&A, MAK, and The Art Institute of Chicago as well as cultural events including the Venice Architecture Biennale. He is Professor of Architecture at UIC, Chicago, visiting professor at Yale School of Architecture, Director of Night School at the Architectural Association and columnist for *Art Review and Dezeen*. Previously he was a founding director of FAT Architecture.

30 Manuel Krebs
Manuel Krebs, graphic designer, works in Zurich.

204 Labics
Labics is an architectural and urban planning practice led by Maria Claudia Clemente and Francesco Isidori. The name of the practice expresses the concept of a laboratory, a testing ground for advanced ideas. Theoretical research and its practical applications form an integral and important part of the practice's work. The research at Labics is geared towards an open, relational and structured architecture, capable of guiding the transformation of a context and of a territory defining new social and urban geographies. Public space, intended as a place of construction and representation of an open and democratic society, always holds a central role in Labics' research, from the more theoretical projects like *Borderline Metropolis* to urban master plans such as La Città del Sole or the Torrespaccata masterplan in Rome, but also in architectural scale projects, like MAST Bologna, Piazza Fontana in Rozzano (MI) and the Italpromo & Libardi Associates headquarters in Rome. In the past few years the office gained several awards, among which the Iconic Award, the Chicago Athenaeum, Inarch-Ance and Dedalo Minosse. In 2015, MAST was shortlisted for the Mies van der Rohe Award. Labics has been invited to participate to several exhibitions, among them the 11th, 12th and 14th Venice Architectural Biennale and the recent monographic exhibition *La Città Aperta* during the Berlin architectural festival *Make City* (2015).

28 Tristan Lavoyer
Tristan Lavoyer, born in 1986, artist, works in Lausanne.

72 Armin Linke
Armin Linke (born 1966, lives in Berlin) combines a range of contemporary image-processing technologies to blur the borders between fiction and reality. His artistic practice is concerned with the interrelations and transformative powers between urban, architectural or spatial functions and the human being's interacting with these environments.

110 Nicholas Lobo Brennan
Nicholas Lobo Brennan is a founding director of APPARATA, a Zurich and London based architecture practice established in 2016. He is the joint editor of the architecture magazine *Models Ruins Power*. He studied architecture at the Royal College of Art and The CASS in London. He has given talks at the Venice Biennale, Delft Berlage, and EPFL amongst other places. He taught at ETH Zurich, at HEAD Geneva and the Gerrit Rietveld Academie Sandburg Institute Amsterdam.

182 Oliver Lütjens
Oliver Lütjens graduated from ETH Zurich in 2002. Before founding Lütjens Padmanabhan Architekten in Zurich with Thomas Padmanabhan in 2007, he worked for Diener & Diener in Basel, Meili Peter Architekten in Zurich and OMA/Rem Koolhaas in Rotterdam. From 2007–2014 he taught as an assistant with Adam Caruso and Peter St John and as head assistant with Adam Caruso at ETH Zurich.

62 Ahmad Makia
Ahmad Makia is a geographer from Dubai. He writes about wet matters, Gulf landscapes, and sex. He also produces books.

78 Martin Marker Larsen
Martin Marker Larsen (born 1987) is an architect and painter. He graduated from the Royal Danish Academy of Fine Arts, School of Architecture, and has worked at the offices of Christ & Gantenbein and Herzog & de Meuron.
Martin is currently teaching at KADK (former Royal Danish Academy of Fine Arts, School of Architecture) in Copenhagen alongside running his own artistic and architectural practice.

122 Nikos Magouliotis
Nikos Magouliotis studied architecture and architectural history & theory in Athens (NTUA) and Oslo (AHO). He is currently working as an assistant and PhD candidate in the ETH/gta, at the Chair of Prof. Maarten Delbeke, in collaboration with the research program "PriArc: Printing the Past. Architecture, Print Culture and Uses of the Past in Modern Europe." He has published texts on the various incarnations and theorizations of the primitive and the vernacular. His current research focuses on the historiography of the vernacular and the byzantine in late nineteenth and early twentieth-century Greece, as it manifests in the field of architectural theory and practice, but also intertwined with similar advances within archaeology and ethnography.

118 Walter Mair
Walter Mair: 1960 born in Zurich, 1980 diploma in photography Kunstgewerbeschule Zurich, 1991 diploma in architecture ETH Zurich.

MOS Architects
MOS Architects is a New York-based architecture studio, founded by principals Hilary Sample and Michael Meredith in 2005. An internationally recognized architecture practice, MOS was the recipient of the 2015 Cooper Hewitt, Smithsonian Design Museum National Design Award in Architecture, the 2010 American Academy of Arts and Letters Architecture Award, and the 2008 Architectural League of New York Emerging Voices Award. Individual works have similarly received numerous awards and distinctions, most notably: the 2015 Global Holcim Award for sustainable construction (Asia-Pacific Region), for Community Center No. 3 (Lali Gurans Orphanage); the cover of *Abitare* and an AIA NY State Award of Excellence, for School No. 1 (Krabbesholm Højskole); the 2014 accession of both the firm's modular, off-grid House No. 5 (Museum of Outdoor Arts Element House) into The Museum of Modern Art, Architecture and Design Collection; the acquisition of House No. 3 (Lot No. 6 / Ordos) into the permanent collection of The Art Institute of Chicago; and the selection of Pavilion No. 4 (Afterparty) for the 2009 MoMA PS1 Young Architects Program. Recent work includes: Store No. 2 (Chamber) in Chelsea, NYC; House No. 10, currently under construction; School No. 2, a competition proposal for the Institute for Advanced Study Commons Building; and Housing No. 4 (Dequindre Cut, Detroit).

Nelson Mota
Nelson Mota is Assistant Professor at TU Delft and guest scholar with The Berlage Center for Advanced Studies in Architecture and Urban Design. He holds a PhD from TU Delft and is a founding partner of comoco arquitectos. He is production editor and member of the editorial board of the academic journal *Footprint*.

Johannes Norlander
Johannes Norlander (1974) studied architecture at Chalmers and KTH in Gothenburg and Stockholm, and graphic design at Stockholm's Konstfack. Between 1996 and 2001, Norlander ran a primarily design-oriented practice. As a designer, he has developed pieces for Asplund, Nola, Collex and HAY. In 2004, Norlander established Johannes Norlander Arkitektur. The practice's first architectural projects were private houses – Älta (2008), Tumle (2009) and Morran (2010). Since 2010, the office has seen the design and construction of two apartment buildings, and won larger-scale commissions like Annex – an addition to Gothenburg's school of economics. The process within the practice is rigorous – never departing from a focus on detail, while working toward layered and multivalent architectural entities. A will to relate to – and mediate – an extended cultural context is at the core of Norlander's work. Smaller-scale projects, teaching and research are crucial elements of the practice. The interplay of projects constitutes a continuous, developing dialogue.

Nicolò Ornaghi
Nicolò Ornaghi (b. 1989), architect. Co-founder of Raumplan, a web platform on visual arts. Through Raumplan studio he designs and produces exhibitions and events. Ornaghi studied at Politecnico di Milano and at AHO (the Oslo School for Architecture and Design). He worked in Salottobuono in Milan, at Spacegroup in Oslo and for Christ & Gantenbein in Basel. He is now living and working in Milan.

Thomas Padmanabhan
Thomas Padmanabhan graduated from Aachen Technical University, Università di Roma "La Sapienza" and Cornell University in 2000. He worked for Skidmore Owings & Merrill in New York, Meili Peter Architekten in Zurich and Diener & Diener Architekten in Basel. In 2007, he founded Lütjens Padmanabhan Architekten in Zurich with Oliver Lütjens. Until 2013, he taught as an assistant with Peter Märkli and Markus Peter at ETH Zurich. Together they taught as visiting critics at TU Munich in 2015 and from 2017 to 2018 they were guest professors at EPF Lausanne.

George Papam Papamattheakis + George Foufas
George Papam Papamattheakis and George Foufas are currently studying at the NTU Athens School of Architecture and have previously studied at the ETH Zurich and BTU Cottbus, respectively. Following an interest in topics concerning urban infrastructures and their spatial influence, this text is a modified excerpt of their dissertation titled *Infrastructure places: The Public Work Through the "system-object" Distinction.*

Daniele Pisani
Daniele Pisani obtained his PhD in History of Architecture at the Università Iuav, Venice, and currently teaches at the Universidade Presbiteriana Mackenzie, São Paulo. Among his publications, *L'architettura è un gesto: Ludwig Wittgenstein architetto* (Macerata, 2011) and *Paulo Mendes da Rocha: Complete Works* (Milano, Barcelona and New York, 2013–2015).

Pedro Pitarch
Pedro Pitarch is an architect (ETSAM, UPM, 2007–2014) and contemporary musician (COM Cáceres 1996–2008). Archiprix International Prize (Hunter Douglas Award 2015), Extraordinary Honour End of Studies Prize at the ETSAM (UPM, 2014) and Superscape2016 Award (Wien, Austria).

He has worked for OMA, Federico Soriano (S&Aa), Burgos+Garrido and collaborated with Izaskun Chinchilla and Andrés Perea. His work has been selected for the 4th Lisbon Architecture Triennale *The World in Our Eyes Exhibition, Architectus Omnibus* curated by Instituto Cervantes/Goethe Institute (Madrid/Berlin), 9th EME3 Festival (Barcelona) and II Un-Conference (Zagreb, ThinkSpace).

He has been shortlisted for the Début Award of the 4th Lisbon Triennale of Architecture. He has received prizes and mentions in international competitions such as: First Prize with "Cultural Factory" for Clesa Building, Honorable Mention at ARCO- madrid2016 VIProom, Special Mention at Jardins de Metis, Honorable Mention for DeArte XIV Contemporary Art Fair Design Space, Honorable Mention at the Past Forward Competition of think tank Think Space.

100 Margarida Quintã

Margarida Quintã (b. 1981, Porto) is an architect. She holds a Diploma in Architecture from the Faculty of Architecture of the University of Porto, and is currently a doctoral candidate at the EPF Lausanne.

106 Philippe Rahm

Philippe Rahm is a Swiss architect, principal in the office of Philippe Rahm architectes, based in Paris, France. His work, which extends the field of architecture from the physiological to the meteorological, has received an international audience in the context of sustainability. He started to teach architecture design at the GSD, Harvard University, USA, in fall 2014. In 2002, Mr. Rahm was chosen to represent Switzerland at the 8th Architecture Biennale in Venice, and was one of the 25 Manifesto's Architects of Aaron Betsky's 2008 Architectural Venice Biennale. He was the 2009 nominee for the Ordos Prize in China and was nominated in 2010 and 2008 for the International Chernikov Prize in Moscow, where he was ranked in the top ten. He has participated in a number of exhibitions worldwide (Archilab, Orléans, France 2000; SF-MoMA 2001; CCA Kitakyushu 2004; Centre Pompidou, Paris, 2003–2006 and 2007; Manifesta 7, 2008; Louisiana Museum, Denmark, 2009; Guggenheim Museum, New York 2010). In 2007, he had a personal exhibition at the Canadian Centre for Architecture in Montreal. Mr. Rahm was a resident at the Villa Medici in Rome (2000). He was Headmaster at the AA School in London in 2005–2006, visiting professor at the Mendrisio Academy of Architecture in Switzerland in 2004 and 2005, at the ETH Lausanne in 2006 and 2007, at the School of Architecture of the Royal Danish Academy of Fine Arts of Copenhagen in 2009–2010, in Oslo at the AHO in 2010–2011. From 2010 to 2012, he held the Jean Labatut Professorship in Princeton University, USA. He has lectured widely, including at Yale, Cooper Union, UCLA and the ETH Zürich. His recent work includes the First Prize for the 70-hectare Taichung Gateway Park in Taiwan (currently under construction), a 13,000 m2 office building at La Défense in France for the EPADESA; a convective condominium for the IBA in Hamburg, Germany; the White Geology, a stage design for contemporary art in the Grand-Palais on the Champs-Elysées in Paris in 2009 and a studio house for the artist Dominique Gonzalez-Foerster in 2008. Monographic books include *Physiological architecture* published by Birkhaüser in 2002, *Distortions,* published by HYX in 2005, *Environ(ne)ment: Approaches for Tomorrow,* published by Skira in 2006, *Architecture Météorologique* published by Archibooks in 2009 and *Constructed Atmospheres* published by Postmedia, Milan, Italy, in 2014.

170 Camilo Rebelo

Born in Porto in 1972, Camilo Rebelo graduated in Architecture from the Faculdade de Arquitectura da Universidade do Porto (FAUP) in 1996. From 1994 to 1999, he collaborated with Eduardo Souto Moura and Herzog & de Meuron.

In 2000 he established his own office. He is a prize-winning author, namely with the first prize in the international competition for the Museum of Art and Archaeology of Vale do Côa (2004–2009), in co-authorship with Tiago Pimentel, later awarded with the Bauwelt Prize 2013 and Douro Architecture Prize 2014. Also awarded with an honorable mention in the international competition for the Museum of Modern Art of Warsaw (2007); nominated to Mies van der Rohe Award (2015) and received the Baku UIA International Award for the Ktima House in Greece (2017), both projects in co-authorship with Susana Martins. Recently nominated for the Mies van der Rohe Award (2018) with "Promise House" project, in co-authorship with Cristina Chicau and Patricio Guedes. Camilo Rebelo lectured at the Faculdade de Arquitectura da Universidade do Porto and as invited professor at École Polytechnique Fédérale de Lausanne together with Eduardo Souto de Moura, at Escuela Técnica Superior de Arquitectura - Universidad de Navarra, at Accademia di Architettura di Mendrisio and currently at Politecnico di Milano - Polo Territoriale di Piacenza.

100 Luís Ribeiro da Silva

Luís Ribeiro da Silva (b. 1982, Porto) is an architect. He holds a Diploma in Architecture from the Faculty of Architecture of the University of Porto, and a Master's degree in Advanced Architectural Design from Columbia University's GSAPP. He is currently a doctoral candidate at the ETH Zurich.

102 Roi Salgueiro Barrio

Roi Salgueiro Barrio (MArch, MDesS, PhD) is a research associate at the MIT Center for Advanced Urbanism, and a member of the editorial team of Actar's UrbanNext platform.

30 Shirana Shahbazi
Shirana Shahbazi, art critic, works in Karachi.

202 Daniela Silva
Daniela Silva is an architect and a researcher. With a career markedly multifaceted and international, she worked in France, Japan, Italy and China. Currently in Lisbon, she divides her professional activity between practice in an architectural studio and the PhD program at ISCTE in the field of Digital Architecture.

98 Giovanna Silva
Giovanna Silva is based in Milan. She worked for *Domus* and *Abitare* as a photographer and photo editor. She is founder of *San Rocco* magazine and Humboldt Books publishing house. She has published several books on her projects, both with Italian and international publishers, among them Mousse Publishing and Bedford Press. Her work has been featured in numerous international exhibitions such as the International Architecture Exhibition (Venezia), NGBK in Berlin, MACRO in Rome, Louisiana Museum in Copenhagen and the Biennials of Istanbul and Thessaloniki.

80 Something Fantastic
Something Fantastic is a design practice founded by three architects, Leonard Streich, Julian Schubert and Elena Schütz. The firm's agenda is based on the idea that architecture is affected by everything and vice versa – affects everything – and therefore, working as architects implies a broad interest and involvement in the world. The studio operates in the extended field of the discipline, aiming to make a difference through smart, touching, simple, prototypical projects.

24 Carolin Stapenhorst
Carolin Stapenhorst studied architecture at RWTH Aachen and IUAV Venice. After her diploma degree at RWTH in 2003, she worked as architect with C+S Associati in Venice. In 2007, she took a PhD grant in Architecture at Polytechnic University of Turin and started her collaboration with Luciano Motta in their own architectural practice, Studio Motta-Stapenhorst. She concluded her doctoral studies in 2012 and was appointed to the Junior Professorship "Tool-Culture" at RWTH Aachen in 2014.

108 Gabriel Tomasulo
Gabriel Tomasulo is a designer based in New England. He is interested in the form and the history of the American built environment, and in how historical understanding can help design better community spaces. His work has appeared in *GSD Platform 8* and has been exhibited in Boston and Hong Kong. He teaches at Boston College.

140 Milica Topalovic
Milica Topalovic is an Assistant Professor of Architecture and Territorial Planning at ETH Zurich. From 2011–15 she studied the city's hinterlands at the ETH Future Cities Laboratory in Singapore. She graduated from the Berlage Institute, and was head of research at the ETH Studio Basel. She is the author of *Belgrade Formal/Informal,* and is currently conducting research on European countryside.

22 Luis Úrculo
Luis Úrculo's work is characterized by his unusual, complex and irreverent portrayal of architecture, both physical and cultural, and the unexpected narratives that arise through the language of his mark making.
As a practicing architect, his work investigates the periphery of the architectural process, the processes, developments and approaches that can be manipulated, sampled and translated into other scales, creating new scenes, experiences and even expectations not contemplated previously. Fiction, representation and interpretation of diverse domestic geographies have been the basis for the development of his practice.
Luis Úrculo has exhibited in the 11th Venice Biennale, The Metropolitan Museum of Art (New York), MAXXI (Roma), Tokyo Wonder Site (Tokyo), MAC Quinta Normal (Santiago, Chile), Art Institute (Chicago), Matadero (Madrid), La Casa Encendida (Madrid), Centro de Arte Tabacalera (Madrid), Fabrica (Lisboa), Arredondo / Arozarena (México), Max Estrella (Madrid), The Popular Workshop (San Francisco), Centro Cultural Estación Mapocho (Chile), Parque Cultural (Valparaiso, Chile), Transculturelles des Abattoirs (Casablanca), National Glyptoteque (Athens), Bienal Iberoamericana de Medellin. As a teacher and researcher, he directs thesis projects with Jaime Hayón for Master of European Design Labs in Istituto Europeo di Design, Madrid.

He has also been invited as visiting professor and lecturer in Genève (HEAD), Columbia University (New York), Danish Center for Architecture (Copenhagen), Vitra Design Museum at Boisbuchet, Kent State University (Florence), Graham Foundation (Chicago), LIGA (Mexico DF), Universidad Anahuac (México), Istanbul Design Biennial, Buenos Aires, Barcelona and Madrid.

100 Ursa
Ursa is an art and architecture studio that creates buildings, objects, images, films and texts. Based in Porto, Portugal, ursa was founded in 2011 out of the shared interests of Alexandre Delmar and Luís Ribeiro da Silva, and is currently led together with Margarida Quintã.

66 Alejandro Valdivieso
Alejandro Valdivieso is an architect and research-

er based in Madrid, currently finishing his doctoral degree (Ph.D.) in the History and Theory of Architecture at the Escuela Técnica Superior de Arquitectura de Madrid (UPM-ETSAM). As a Fulbright Scholar, he received a Post-Professional Master's degree in Design Studies in History and Philosophy of Design from Harvard University Graduate School of Design. Valdivieso develops his work through different formats and media: as an active practicing architect, as writer and editor for several platforms and as an educator; currently an Assistant Professor of Architectural History & Theory at UPM-ETSAM in Madrid.

78 Christian Vennerstrøm Jensen
Christian Vennerstrøm Jensen (b. 1988) graduated from The Royal Danish Academy of Fine Arts, School of Architecture in Copenhagen. While working with Studio Anne Holtrop from 2015–2018 he co-founded "bahraini – danish," an architecture studio named after the many overlapping moments in history between Denmark and Bahrain, amongst them the continuous excavation of the Royal Mounds in A'ali lead by Danish archaeologists. Photography continues to be a means to see and understand his extended surroundings.

130 WAI Architecture
WAI Architecture Think Tank practices architecture from a panoramic approach. Founded in Brussels in 2008 by Cruz Garcia and Nathalie Frankowski, WAI is currently based in Beijing, Taliesin and Taliesin West where both directors are Visiting Teaching Fellows at the Frank Lloyd Wright School of Architecture.

58 Ala Younis
Ala Younis is an artist, trained as architect, with research, curatorial, film and publishing projects. She presented *Plan for Greater Baghdad* (2015) at 56th Venice Biennale's *All the World's Futures,* and *An Index of Tensional and Unintentional Love of Land* at The New Museum (2014). She curated Kuwait's first national pavilion at the 55th Venice Biennale (2013), and the "Museum of Manufactured Response to Absence" (2012–). Younis is co-founder of the non-profit publishing initiative Kayfa ta.

84 Camille Zakharia
Camille Zakharia graduated with a Bachelor of Fine Arts from NSCAD University Halifax Canada in 1997 and a Bachelor of Engineering from the American University of Beirut in 1985. Zakharia has exhibited prolifically across North America, Europe and the Middle East, including the Venice Biennale Italy, the Victoria & Albert Museum, London, UK; Canadian Museum of Civilization, Quebec, Canada and Musee du Quai Branly, Paris, France.

190 Raphael Zuber
Raphael Zuber studied architecture until 2001 at the Swiss Federal Institute of Technology Zurich (ETHZ) and opened his own office in the same year. His first building is the Schoolhouse Grono. In 2016 he completed his second one, the Apartment Building in Domat/Ems. Among his important projects are the Ethnographic Museum Neuchâtel, the university campus SUPSI in Mendrisio and the Weekend House on the Isle of Harris in Scotland. Raphael Zuber has taught at several architecture schools, including the Accademia di Architettura di Mendrisio, the Oslo School of Architecture and Design and the EPFL in Lausanne.

94 Cino Zucchi
Cino Zucchi graduated from MIT and the Politecnico di Milano, where he teaches. He has been Visiting Professor at the Harvard GSD, president of the jury of the Mies van der Rohe Award 2015, and curator of the 2014 Italian Pavilion at the Venice Biennale. Among his realized projects the Junghans renewal in Venice, the Alfa Romeo area in Milan and the Lavazza HQ in Turin.

The 2016 cycle CARTHA *on The Form of Form* is the result of the work and support of many generous people and institutions. First, we would like to thank the 2016 Lisbon Architecture Triennale team for having selected our proposal as an Associated Project and for their trust in our commitment to dedicate one year of editorial activity to the topic of form in architecture. Furthermore, we would like to thank André Tavares, Chief Curator of the 2016 Lisbon Architecture Triennale, for his precise words in the preface that provide the appropriate context and intellectual framework of the work presented in this book.

We would also like to thank the guest editors of Issue I *How to Learn Better* – Leopold Banchini and Daniel Zamarbide – as well as the guest editors of Issue II *The Architecture of the City. A Palimpsest* – Victoria Easton, Matilde Cassani, and Noura Al-Sayeh. Their generous acceptance of our invitation and enthusiasm brought an otherwise impossible richness of ideas, quality and outreach to the cycle.

The content of this book was officially presented at the exhibition *CARTHA on The Form of Form* held in December 2016 in Lisbon at the Museu da Água – Mãe d'Àgua das Amoreiras Reservoir. We would like to thank the Museu da Água, the Fundação Serra Henriques and the Swiss Arts Council Pro Helvetia for their support of this exhibition at the 2016 Lisbon Architecture Triennale. Likewise, we would like to thank Gonçalo Frias, Max Frischknecht and Esther Lohri for their help during both the organization of this exhibition and the editorial cycle of 2016.

The book *CARTHA on The Form of Form* has been made possible thanks to the generosity of various public and private companies and institutions. CARTHA is profoundly thankful for their uncompromised support.

Finally, our most sincere gratitude and recognition is for the authors of the content presented in this book. We proudly acknowledge their willingness to react to our call for papers and to accept our invitations. It is only through their generosity to share their work that CARTHA is able to generate a collective critical dialogue about architecture, open to all.

Contributors:
Åbäke
Noura Al Sayeh
ALICE / Dieter Dietz
Amateur Cities
Annette Amberg
Pier Vittorio Aureli
Babau Bureau
Pau Bajet
Titi Balali
Patricia Barbas
Shumon Basar
Baukuh
Laura Bonell
Bureau A
Adrià Carbonell
Matilde Cassani
Ciriacidis Lenherer Architekten
José Pedro Cortes
Laura Cristea
Irina Davidovici
Andrea Alberto Dutto
Victoria Easton
Edelaar Mosayebi Inderbitzin Architekten
Mariabruna Fabrizi
Farquet Architectes
Simona Ferrari
George Foufas
GANKO
Cloé Gattigo
Stefano Graziani
Owen Hatherley
Studio Anne Holtrop
Sam Jacob
Manuel Krebs
Labics
Tristan Lavoyer
Armin Linke
Nicholas Lobo Brennan
Daniel López-Dóriga
Fosco Lucarelli
Lütjens Padmanabhan Architekten
Nikos Magouliotis
Walter Mair
Ahmad Makia
Martin Marker Larsen
MOS Architects
Nelson Mota
Johannes Norlander Arkitektur AB
Nicolò Ornaghi
George Papam Papamattheakis
Daniele Pisani
Pedro Pitarch
Philippe Rahm
Camilo Rebelo
Roi Salgueiro Barrio
Shirana Shahbazi
Daniela Silva
Giovanna Silva
Something Fantastic
Carolin Stapenhorst
Milica Topalovic
Gabriel Tomasulo
Luis Úrculo
URSA
Alejandro Valdivieso
Christian Vennerstrom
Wai Think Tank / Cruz Garcia & Nathalie Frankowski
Ala Younis
Camille Zakharia
Raphael Zuber
Cino Zucchi

CARTHA Editorial Board:
Elena Chiavi
Pablo Garrido Arnaiz
Matilde Girão
Francisco Moura Veiga
Francisco Ramos Ordóñez
Brittany Utting
Rubén Valdez

Proofreading:
Nathalie Üstünay

Graphic Design:
Début Début (Max Frischknecht & Philipp Möckli)
www.debutdebut.com

Institutional Support:
Fundação Serra Henriques
Pro Helvetia – Swiss Arts Council

Sponsors:
Magizan Architecture et Urbanisme
Burckhardt+Partner Architekten AG
RAPP Architekten AG
ZPF Ingenieure AG

Printer:
Gugler, Melk

Font:
Funktional Grotesk

Paper:
Euroboard Spezial GT2
Munken Print White

Efforts have been made to correct factual and grammatical errors and to standardize typographical elements. Eccentricities of language and phrasing have been retained.

Authors, editors and publisher have made every reasonable attempt to contact copyright holders. Should mistakes have occurred thereby, claims will be satisfied in due process.

Copyright
© 2019 CARTHA and Park Books, Zurich
© for the texts: the authors
© for the images: the authors

All rights reserved; no part of this publication may be reproduced, stored in a retrieval system or transmitted in any form or by any means, electronic, mechanical, photocopying, recording, or otherwise, without the prior written consent of the publisher.

www.carthamagazine.com
info@carthamagazine.com

Publisher:
Park Books
Niederdorfstrasse 54
8001 Zurich
Switzerland
www.park-books.com

Park Books is being supported by the Federal Office of Culture with a general subsidy for the years 2016–2020.

ISBN 978-3-03860-070-1